PRAISE FOR *TRUE RICHES*

"I know and love Greg Baumer and John Cortines. I admire their hearts for God and their grasp of what money is, and of what financial stewardship means. I'm grateful that the good news about generous giving has so touched their lives. Greg and John are enthusiastic and articulate concerning life-changing truths. I really enjoyed *True Riches* and I believe you will too."

—Randy Alcorn, author of *The Treasure Principle*, *Managing God's Money*, and *Money, Possessions, and Eternity*

"*True Riches* is a superb book by any measure. It is artfully written, thoroughly biblical, wonderfully practical, and incredibly motivating. I couldn't put it down, because it so clearly articulates God's heart for how we are to joyfully handle money and possessions. I believe it's destined to become a classic and heartily recommend it!"

—Howard Dayton, founder of Compass

"I deeply admire John and Greg for not only giving us this thoughtful new perspective on how to truly honor God with our money and possessions, but for also transparently sharing their own journeys of discovery and learning. Rather than just accepting conventional Christian wisdom on this all-important topic (which often amounts to slapping 'a Christian halo over the American dream'), they share fresh and powerful insights into biblical truth, and then give us practical tools to evaluate our own personal financial picture. But this is not about guilt-tripping us into ever-more-responsible stewardship. Instead, John and Greg illustrate how God is inviting us on a rewarding adventure of faith, to partner with him to fulfill his kingdom, and to grow spiritually in the process. Whether you just got your first paycheck or have managed wealth for many years, you need to read this wonderfully inspiring book that challenges us to rethink how our relationship with our money is really affecting our hearts, our world, and our relationship with God."

—Wess Stafford, president emeritus of
Compassion International

"*True Riches* invites us to find freedom and joy in our finances by daily living out the teachings of Jesus. Practical, engaging, and countercultural, this concise guide will help you to move from a posture of anxiety to contentment, and from worry to generosity. For those seeking an eternal perspective on money, this book is a must-read!"

—Peter Greer, president and CEO of HOPE
International and coauthor of *Mission Drift*

"John and Greg live their talk. They are open and honest about their struggles and wins and are thoroughly biblical in their approach, as well as humble and wise beyond their years. *True Riches* challenges winsomely without prefab formulas. I highly recommend this work."

—Robert L. Plummer, PhD, chairman of the
Southern Baptist Theological Seminary's
New Testament Department

"*True Riches* is a book that will challenge you to rethink your perspective on money and giving. It is both encouraging and convicting. I am grateful for the work of John Cortines and Greg Baumer. Their insight into God's perspective on money is useful for Christians everywhere. I recommend this book to anyone who is ready to have their financial lives redirected in a God-centered way."

—Dr. Evan Lenow, professor at Southwestern
Baptist Theological Seminary

"*True Riches* is a powerful book that presents a biblical framework for practically experiencing the life that is truly life. It is thought-provoking while being easy to read. I have found myself thinking about the book consistently since finishing it and praying for the qualities Greg and John present in the book to develop in my life on the pathway to *true riches*."

—Todd Harper, president of Generous Giving

"*True Riches* blends biblical insight with practical information to create a helpful handbook on financial management—for *everyone*. John and Greg are sincere, earnest, and devoted while also remaining honestly realistic and approachable. So, whether you're just starting to consider the role of money in your life, or you're well down the financial road, you'll find help and hope here."

—Elisa Morgan, president emerita of MOPS International, cohost of *Discover the Word*, and author of *The Prayer Coin*

TRUE
RICHES

WHAT JESUS REALLY SAID
ABOUT MONEY AND
YOUR HEART

John Cortines & Gregory Baumer

NELSON
BOOKS
An Imprint of Thomas Nelson

Published in Nashville, Tennessee, by Nelson Books, an imprint of Thomas Nelson. Nelson Books and Thomas Nelson are registered trademarks of HarperCollins Christian Publishing, Inc.

Thomas Nelson titles may be purchased in bulk for educational, business, fund-raising, or sales promotional use. For information, please e-mail SpecialMarkets@ ThomasNelson.com.

Unless otherwise noted, Scripture quotations are taken from the ESV® Bible (The Holy Bible, English Standard Version®). Copyright © 2001 by Crossway, a publishing ministry of Good News Publishers. Used by permission. All rights reserved.

Scripture quotations marked THE MESSAGE are from *The Message*. Copyright © by Eugene H. Peterson 1993, 1994, 1995, 1996, 2000, 2001, 2002. Used by permission of NavPress. All rights reserved. Represented by Tyndale House Publishers, Inc.

Scripture quotations marked NIV are from the Holy Bible, New International Version®, NIV®. Copyright © 1973, 1978, 1984, 2011 by Biblica, Inc.® Used by permission of Zondervan. All rights reserved worldwide. www.Zondervan.com. The "NIV" and "New International Version" are trademarks registered in the United States Patent and Trademark Office by Biblica, Inc.®

Any Internet addresses, phone numbers, or company or product information printed in this book are offered as a resource and are not intended in any way to be or to imply an endorsement by Thomas Nelson, nor does Thomas Nelson vouch for the existence, content, or services of these sites, phone numbers, companies, or products beyond the life of this book.

ISBN 978-1-4002-0854-8 (eBook)
ISBN 978-1-4002-0853-1 (HC)

Library of Congress Control Number: 2018964221

Printed in the United States of America
19 20 21 22 23 LSC 10 9 8 7 6 5 4 3 2 1

To Megan. We've come to learn about the joys and the costs of discipleship together, but you've never wavered in your love and dedication to our King and the true riches he offers. You're my best friend, the love of my life, editor, speaking coach, and a loving mother to our children. I fall more in love with you every year!—John

To Alison. You inspire me every day with your gracious, selfless generosity. Your consistent, sacrificial love is an immeasurable blessing to me, our children, and our community. I thank God daily for convincing you to marry me! I look forward to continuing to serve the Lord together with you. I love you!—Greg

CONTENTS

FOREWORD

"DO YOU TRUST ME?"

This is a big question from God that we must answer in every area of life. The Christian life is supposed to be lived by faith! In this book, John and Greg invite us to apply real faith and trust to our finances. They invite us to consider that trusting God and walking by faith could be the most joyful, adventurous, and eternally rewarding path we can follow with our money. This runs contrary to the popular belief, even in Christian circles, that managing money is all about responsibility—formulas, steps, and crafting a perfect plan. Those things matter, but they fall short of the full invitation of Jesus in this area of our lives. At the end of the day, we are called to take new steps of faith on an adventure with God.

My life verse is Proverbs 3:5–6: "Trust in the LORD with all your heart, and do not lean on your own understanding. In all your ways acknowledge him, and he will make straight your paths." This verse and the question of trust in God has defined my football journey. God never promised me success; he just asked me to trust him and walk with him day by day. He asked me to trust him when I broke my ankle as a high school quarterback, potentially ending my shot at getting recruited to play in college. He asked me to trust him when I had no scholarship offers at the end of my senior season in high school, and again when my prospects of becoming the starting quarterback at Michigan State appeared slim throughout my freshman and sophomore years.

After a successful college career, I had hopes of being drafted to the NFL in the first or second round, but God asked me to trust him when I fell to the fourth round and got drafted to a team where I would surely be just a backup. It would be three years before I became the starting quarterback for the Washington Redskins. Through years of uncertainty and contract negotiations, I tried to always trust in God's sovereign control over my life. As this book goes to press, it is now my privilege to be the starting quarterback for the Minnesota Vikings. Through it all, God continues to invite me to trust him and walk in relationship with him each step of the way, in football and in life.

The point of my football journey is not that trusting God brings amazing success. Rather, in success or failure, in great moments and in weak moments, my highest calling and opportunity is to grow in my walk with him. I've navigated life without much money as a college student and am now navigating life with abundant finances. My wife, Julie, and I have learned to walk in a trusting relationship with God in this area of our lives. We firmly believe that money itself is neither good nor bad, but its use is highly spiritual! There are no easy answers, but there is a faithful God who invites us to humbly walk with him through every financial circumstance and decision.

Here are a few lessons Julie and I have learned, lessons that are also woven into the book you hold:

- God owns it all. (Ps. 50)
- The power to make wealth comes from God, not ourselves. (Deut. 8:18)
- Giving is an investment in eternity. (Matt. 6:20)
- You can't out-give God!

When I was seventeen, I heard Gary Haugen, the founder of International Justice Mission (IJM), speak on God's heart for bringing justice to the oppressed. I was moved and prayed that God would someday bless me with money so that I could invest in the amazing work of the organization. I could never have imagined that roughly a decade later, I would launch my NFL career in Washington, DC, the city where IJM is headquartered! Being a part of IJM's work—and the work of many other amazing ministries—has been one of Julie's and my greatest joys. We pray that God might allow us to use all he gives us for his glory, as we trust him day by day.

May I never put my hope and security in a paycheck or a bank balance but in God, who faithfully provides. I want to leave a legacy for him and his kingdom, and he calls you to the same. I know he has a plan for you and asks you to trust him in the ways that John and Greg will describe in the pages to come. This book is an invitation to that journey of trust and faithfulness. May we all join together in this adventure with God.

He asks each of us, "Do you trust me?" I pray that our hearts and lives will all answer with a resounding, "YES!"

—Kirk Cousins, NFL quarterback

INTRODUCTION

Discovering True Riches

FINANCIAL SUCCESS is never as fulfilling as we think it will be. When money controls our decisions, we find momentary satisfaction but lasting discontent. When God controls our decisions, we find momentary challenges but lasting peace.

God, in his grace, allowed me (John) to realize this at age twenty-six, and my life has never been the same. I let go of money as the secret master of my life, and I discovered more adventure, deeper emotions, and a closer and more fulfilling fellowship with God than I had ever known to be possible.

Until then I had diligently followed every wise financial rule, even from childhood. I had saved up $10,000 mowing lawns in the blazing summer heat as a high schooler. I had studied hard to land a great job and earned six figures in my first year out of college. My wife and I tithed faithfully and saved like crazy, amassing $300,000 in savings by the time we were both twenty-four. I headed to Harvard Business School in further pursuit of this financial mission and successfully landed an offer for my post-MBA dream job. After graduation my wife and I would be headed overseas, where I'd earn more than $300,000 per year.

We planned to save up enough money so that when we came back to the United States, we could pay cash for a house and avoid a mortgage altogether.

But then, in his mercy and goodness, God started revealing to me the emptiness of my life in pursuit of money. Sitting in our Boston apartment on a cold, snowy day, I slowly read the twelfth chapter of Luke's gospel over and over, and the words of Jesus pierced my heart. I began to realize that, even though I had met every financial goal I had ever set, I was chasing the wind. I felt God asking me if I would consider a different kind of life: a life of joyful freedom, deep sacrifice, and heartfelt trust. In the months after that wintry day I spent with Luke 12, my wife and I prepared to change our life trajectory forever.

At first we thought we would still take my dream job, go overseas, and begin giving half of our earnings away instead of saving so aggressively. But in a clear and compelling way, God began to reveal that he wanted us to abandon our dreams and instructing me to take a job with a small nonprofit organization instead. It meant a 65 percent pay cut. It meant student loans and a mortgage for the next decade or two instead of being debt-free. It meant that we couldn't send our kids to elite private schools. And it could mean career suicide. But God was relentless and clear that this was his plan.

As we wrestled with God, we asked him big questions. "Why would you call us away from our dream that we worked so hard for? Can we really trust you? Why do we feel upset, even angry, even in the midst of truly following your call?"

We counted the cost of following Jesus, and the cost was high.[1] But we also couldn't deny what we were being called to do. So we paid the cost in broken dreams, tears, and countless moments of doubt. It wasn't quite like the fairy-tale stories of discipleship where—after a bold step of faith—sunshine and rainbows erupt everywhere as we joyfully sing praise songs. Instead, while we knew we were squarely in the middle of God's will, we felt isolated, spiritually attacked, and alone for two full years.

But we eventually discovered that the joy of walking with God is worth any price we might have to pay. In hindsight my wife and I can now say that we have experienced the rich abundance of a life of intimacy with him. We wouldn't trade our journey of surrender for anything else.

THE CONVERSATION WE'RE NOT HAVING

I didn't realize until later on that, in leading me away from a high-paying job overseas, God had actually been protecting me. Unknowingly, I had made an idol out of stability and security, and deep down I believed that financial success was a hallmark of a life well lived. Often in the Bible, however, financial success is seen in a mixed light. It's a blessing from God, yes, but it's also tremendously dangerous. In fact, Jesus said it would be very difficult for financially successful people to gain access to his kingdom! By asking me to lay down my financial stability, God was teaching me that my personal worth as a human being did not come from my financial net worth. Because of my hardness of heart, it was a lesson he needed to teach me the hard way.

Unfortunately, despite my Christian upbringing, I was never taught about financial issues in church. Real, honest dialogue about faith and finances is rare. For some reason the two seem to be allergic to each other. We typically don't talk about money with our spiritual mentors or think about our faith when we're paying off a student loan or buying a house. On the rare day that we learn about money in church, we usually hear about a formulaic life plan that looks something like this:

Get out of debt. Achieve home ownership. Save for retirement. Live a comfortable, secure life. Just be sure to give 10 percent of your income away. Follow this path faithfully, and you'll become stable and secure—maybe even rich.

This formula basically teaches us to do exactly what the culture around us does, with a special emphasis on staying debt-free and giving 10 percent away. It puts a nice, Christian halo over the American dream. This is the formula I had been following, thinking I was being a great Christian role model with my financial life. But when my friend Greg and I started looking more closely at the teachings of Jesus, we could not find a single reference to anything like this formula, despite how frequently he taught about money. We had a hunch that something was missing.

To validate this hunch, we conducted a formal survey of the eighty most knowledgeable experts we could find on this subject. The list included seminary professors, business leaders, stewardship pastors, senior pastors, financial advisors, and ministry leaders, many of whom have spent their whole lives studying and teaching what the Bible says about money.

Specifically, we asked these leaders if they were satisfied with how the typical churchgoer is equipped with a biblical perspective on money. The result? Only one of them answered yes. In elections a 60 percent vote is considered a landslide victory. In this case we had 99 percent of experts agreeing that things are not going well when it comes to our understanding of God and money. This is an oversight with far-reaching consequences.

We Christians desperately need a firm foundation for faith and finances, or we risk missing out on the fullness of all that God has for us. Greg and I wrote this book in hopes of making a small contribution toward this much-needed conversation. We've tried to build a firm foundation of content rooted in the teachings of God. We've also formatted this book so it is easy to journey with others and to stir up conversations among those who feel they can't find contentment or peace, no matter how good they get at saving or living responsibly. If your church gave you this book, it's because they want to become a place where people can learn life-giving truths about money, overcoming the isolation and disappointment that are all too common.

Ultimately, this is for people willing to go after the treasure of the kingdom of God. Are you willing to abandon everything you thought you knew about money and stewardship in pursuit of the overflowing joy Jesus offers? You may not need to change careers like I did, but we hope this book can light the way as you consider embracing Jesus' teachings about money, however that may look in your own life. His calling is never easy, but following him is the most rewarding journey we can imagine.

1

THE BIG
QUESTION

A TWENTY-THREE-YEAR-OLD INVESTMENT banker gives half of his income away rather than saving or spending his earnings. A couple in their seventies gives away their retirement nest egg. A father can't fully cover his kids' college expenses because his family has been so generous to God's work through the years. A woman of modest means gives away her car savings fund to a widow in need. An entrepreneur gives his company away.

These are the stories of people we've met as we've traveled the country having conversations about faith and finances. They are shocking and challenging and may leave you feeling uneasy. To be honest, they make us uneasy, too, because these decisions seem foolish on the surface. They seem to go against the basic principles of financial wisdom we've all absorbed through the years. In a conversation about stewardship, the concept of "letting go" in this way, of opening yourself up to such radical giving, grates against how we've been taught, the status quo. But, if we look at the unique level of peace and joy visible in these people's lives, perhaps it's not so crazy after all.

We don't all have to live exactly like these radical givers, but we do all have to answer the critically important question that started them on their paths: *How are my finances shaping my heart?*

As we'll see, that question is the one Jesus cared about most when it came to money. It was also the one question neither of us had ever asked before we met and became friends in graduate school.

We both grew up hearing in church and in our culture that we should save a lot, give steadily, and spend what we want, as long as it is within our means. According to this formula, we each got off to a successful start. We were earning six-figure salaries and tithing regularly by our early twenties—the picture of what financial faithfulness is supposed to look like. Despite our outward success, however, a gnawing, almost invisible sense of unease remained. If we were succeeding financially, why did it not feel more fulfilling?

My wife and I (John) realized that our desire to save obsessively reflected a need to keep score with our bank account, and we had idolized security. We even looked down on people who were "less responsible" with money. My aggressive saving had filled my heart with both pride and anxiety—there was always another financial milestone to chase. And chasing those milestones was keeping me from experiencing the joy of generosity.

Meanwhile, my wife and I (Greg) realized that our desire to live life to the fullest, through spending on great experiences and possessions, reflected an inner belief that we could find greater satisfaction in our stuff than in our Savior. We may have been living within our means, but this false belief was thwarting my relationship with God and was actually granting me less satisfaction, not more.

Despite our outward pictures of success, our financial perspectives represented spiritual failure and were keeping us from maximizing the joyful relationship with God that Jesus was inviting us to. Remember the one key question we should all be asking: *How are my finances shaping my heart?* Well, the answer for us was not pretty. The peace and joy we truly wanted eluded us. Our financial postures were driving us further from God.

WHAT JESUS SAID

If we want to live the best, happiest, and most purposeful lives possible, we need to look to the teachings of Jesus in the Bible. Money was a central theme in many of his teachings and parables. This is consistent with the Bible as a whole, which contains around 2,350 verses pertaining to money, possessions, and our attitude toward them. Contrary to most of what we hear about money today, Jesus' road map for an abundant financial life was *not* to ensure that everyone would become well-off. In fact, even though financial wealth and stability seem to be good things, we have no record of Jesus encouraging us to pursue them. Not even once![1] Rather, he taught about money to inspire people toward a closer relationship with God, whom he referred to as "our Father." Personal finance to him was not an issue of following financial rules; it was about a dynamic relationship of trust with God, a journey toward the riches that are ultimately the most fulfilling.

Our handling of money can lead us to the true riches of a deeper relationship with Jesus himself, marked by *gratitude*, *contentment*, *trust*, and *love*. But if we pursue money for its own sake, we're chasing false riches, and our lives will become marked by *pride*, *coveting*, *anxiety*, and *indifference*, fostering a tragic separation from God and the joy he offers. Thus, Jesus' teachings focus less on the attainment of wealth and more on how our relationship with money forms our character.

Interestingly, many of the financially stable and diligent characters we find in the Bible were condemned specifically for their attitudes toward money. King Shallum, Ananias and Sapphira, the rich fool, the rich young ruler, the rich man from the story of Lazarus, and the entire church in Laodicea come to mind as a few examples. Any of them could have been a success story found in *Money Magazine*, but in God's eyes they failed. They pursued money for its own sake, neglecting their opportunities to serve God and others financially, and this resulted in judgment. Yes, there are some wealthy leaders who are commended (such as Lydia, Cornelius, and Zacchaeus), but they seem to be the exception rather than the rule.

As is illustrated in Scripture, money is a deceptive force that can capture people's hearts, drawing them away from God like a powerful magnet. The closer you get to a magnet, the harder it pulls—and the more you give your heart to money, the more ensnared you will become. In fact, Jesus identified money as the primary competitor for the affections of the human heart when he said, "No one can serve two masters. . . . You cannot serve God and money."[2]

We would be wise to heed the warning coming from the lives of these people in the Bible. Even if we are responsible and diligent, have perfectly updated budgets on Mint.com, and are steadily saving for retirement, we can still fail spiritually when it comes to managing what we've been given.

CULTURE CLASH

When the Pharisees, a group of religious leaders, heard Jesus' teachings on money, they made fun of him. We can visualize the scene: The well-dressed and educated leaders are standing together under the pleasant shade of a palm tree. Luke, the doctor who wrote a history of Jesus' life, called these men "lovers of money."[3] Their beards are neatly trimmed, and they have new, well-fitting robes and nice leather sandals. Perhaps one leans toward his friend with a cynical frown and remarks,

> Why do people listen to this guy? He just panders to the masses with this financial jibber-jabber. Sell your possessions and give to the poor? Yeah, right. Who would take care of you then? It is more blessed to give than to receive? Convenient thing to teach people when you're a poor, traveling preacher. I can't believe this guy. I've worked hard to earn my keep, and have been saving for ten years to buy a property I can retire on. I give my tithe, but come on! If I listened to this guy I'd never be able to make it.

Jesus responded with a strong rebuke: "God knows your hearts. For what is exalted among men is an abomination in the sight of God."

An abomination! These were strong words from Jesus, aimed at the financial wisdom of his time—and ours. Jesus clashed with the natural human mind-set toward money and issued stern warnings toward all who espoused it.

This story hit painfully close to home for us. As young professionals we had so easily absorbed our culture's posture toward money—a posture that would lead us away from the God we wanted to know and serve. Our financial perspective went something like this:

I'm proud of what I've accomplished in life. I've worked hard and deserve a few nice things. I see what other people have—houses, cars, and comfortable lifestyles—and these inspire my desires. I'm driven to save and invest by my concerns about the future. And even though I know there are people with needs, I've got to look after myself and my family before I can help anyone else.

Sound familiar? Without knowing it, we, like the Pharisees, dutifully pursued the false riches of money for its own sake, which led us toward pride, coveting, anxiety, and indifference. A person on this path, even if rich, is truly poor within.

Jesus, however, invites us to consider a radically different posture, reflected in the following paragraph:

I'm grateful for all I have. It is all truly a gift I never deserved! Though I have some goals and dreams, I'm totally content, even in times of suffering, because my identity is secure in Jesus. In every situation, I lean on God and trust him for provision, although my own planning and hard work plays a role. My heart and my life are full of generosity, animated by love for those in need, even when it costs me dearly.

Inviting Christ into our financial journeys makes all the difference in the world. A person on this path, even if poor, is truly rich within. It's a path that completely changes our attitudes and behaviors, molding our hearts into ones filled with the joy, peace, and fulfillment we're all looking for.

The remainder of this book is built around the four joy-filled transformations that are a part of our financial journeys with Christ. In these transformations, we leave behind false riches and acquire true riches. These traits, and the behaviors that spring from them, represent the difference between spiritual success and spiritual failure when it comes to money. In fact, these traits help us look a lot more like the master of generosity, Jesus himself—full of purpose and joy no matter our circumstances. So come along with us, and let's get started.

We move from **Pride** to **Gratitude**
and therefore, we **See Everything As a Gift**.

We move from **Coveting** to **Contentment**
and therefore, we **Spend Modestly**.

We move from **Anxiety** to **Trust**
and therefore, we **Save Modestly**.

We move from **Indifference** to **Love**
and therefore, we **Give Extravagantly**.

APPLICATION: JOURNEYING THROUGH THIS BOOK

In 2013, we (Greg and John) didn't know each other. By 2015, we were best friends. This dramatic swing happened as we began to explore biblical generosity and stewardship together. We know—it's a weird thing to bond over.

While our experience is probably extreme, we hope you find others to discuss this book with and other ways to prayerfully consider the topics at hand. In our own journeys to follow Jesus financially, we would have given up long ago if not for encouragement from each other, our spouses, and many other like-minded peers. We all need friends who will join us in our pursuit of true riches.

We also would have given up if our journeys had not

been supplemented by pen-to-paper planning, prayer, and a posture of worship. For this reason we've built the book to incorporate all these success factors. You can read straight through to the end, but our experience suggests that if you stop to discuss with a friend, fill out a pen-to-paper exercise, or sit in worship before God, you will be even more encouraged and strengthened for the journey.

Take a moment now to consider who you might share your journey to true riches with. Feel free to write their names below or in your own journal.

_____

_____

_____

_____

If you do find some friends to journey with, or if you're already part of a small group focused on this book, you can find the group guide in the back, complete with agendas for each of the four sessions. All songs, videos, and resources—including the exercises at the end of each chapter—are embedded for free at www.truerichesbook.com. You can write your responses to the exercises in the book or use your own journal.

These light bulbs appear throughout the book and represent best practices and practical tips for seeking true riches. We hope they're helpful in your journey.

2

FROM PRIDE TO GRATITUDE

Preserve gratitude like a precious deposit within your soul, and from it you will receive a double portion of delight.

—*Basil of Caesarea*

We move from Pride to Gratitude
We move from Coveting to Contentment
We move from Anxiety to Trust
We move from Indifference to Love

KUDZU IS A weed that was introduced to the southeastern United States more than one hundred years ago as a shade plant for porches. It quickly broke loose and began expanding its foothold, claiming millions of acres in the ensuing decades. Today, we can't seem to rid ourselves of this invasive weed, and it costs hundreds of millions of dollars per year in lost forest productivity. Mowing and hacking are some of the best methods to control it, reducing the weed chop by chop, but it almost always comes back.

Pride in our hearts is a bit like kudzu. It's in there, even if we've recently chopped it down to size. When we least expect it, it might pop back up again. We begin to imagine it is our own efforts that have brought about the good things in our lives. We can hack away at our pride, but only a true experience of God's grace can conquer this pest. Without that, pride swallows up our gratitude, robbing us of the joy of God's unmerited favor in much the same way kudzu covers the beautiful foliage of the American South.

In his book *Mere Christianity*, C. S. Lewis notes that "Pride is spiritual cancer: it eats up the very possibility of love, or contentment, or even common sense."[1] Many of the church fathers taught that pride is the queen of all the vices, the most diabolical of sins, the dark wellspring of all other evils in the human heart. When we put our confidence in ourselves rather than the One who created us, we become puffed up and develop a warped perspective. If, on the other hand, we view our gracious God as the source of all good things, our hearts swell not with pride but with gratitude and joy.

Embracing gratitude over pride is therefore the first step toward experiencing the joy of God in our finances. While it may feel less practical or less simple to immediately apply in our money management, the move toward gratitude will enable us to experience much more success in aligning our money with God's plan in the chapters to come. Gratitude undergirds and supports contentment, trust, and love in the same way a foundation holds up a house. It may be invisible most of the time, but without it the house won't stay standing for long.

MY PRIDE AND YOURS

What is your greatest lifetime accomplishment? Most of us can quickly come up with a list of contenders. Perhaps we think of our jobs, our families, or our possessions. We live in a culture that celebrates individual accomplishments. The self-made man is our icon of success. It's true that most of our greatest achievements—graduations, big promotions, paying off our houses—involve some very hard work on our parts. But we live in a complex ecosystem of connected factors; nothing is solely due to our own efforts.

Just think about earning money at your job. Your skills were given by God (Ps. 144:1). Your job itself is a gift from God (Ex. 20:9), and the political order under which your company has license to operate is ordained by God (Rom. 13:1–2). Even the planet you stand upon has the precise mixture of gases you need for breathing and the optimal temperature for you to live, while offering an atmospheric shield from deadly cosmic rays. The whole universe is held together each moment by the gracious hand of God (Col. 1:17). Not to mention your parents, teachers, coaches, friends, pastors, and countless other people who invested in you at critical moments of your life—they are a gift from God too!

Take out any number of these factors, and your accomplishments would simply disappear. Reflecting on the fragility of our successes—how contingent they are—frees us to let go of pride and say thank you to the God who made them possible. He is the factor most central to it all. Our economy assigns wealth and income to individuals, but if we get caught up in thinking that money is generated by our own isolated efforts, we deceive ourselves into the trap of pride. Far better to recognize every dollar as a gift from our gracious Father—a precious gift to be treasured, stewarded, and shared.

The idea that we cannot stand on our own is at the heart of the Christian faith. You and I alone couldn't get the job done spiritually, ethically, or socially. Most of us have heard the verse, "All have sinned and fall short of the glory of God."[2] It's true! Only in Jesus are we made complete, and he is the source of the air in our lungs, the money in our bank accounts, and the true riches of life in relationship with God—now and for eternity.

But our sense of self-sufficiency, our pride, is hard to admit, and it too often creeps in slowly and stealthily, as we can see in the story of David.

David was the greatest and most famous king of ancient Israel. His life was amazingly complex and full of intrigue, drama, and adventure—the stuff of a Hollywood movie plot. He beheaded a giant, narrowly dodged spears hurled in his direction, and once danced nearly naked through the streets in jubilant celebration. He was an intellectual, too, becoming the number-one bestselling author of poetry in world history.[3] He faced many moments of despair but kept an unwavering faith that God was both the sovereign king of the world and the author of his own life story. What a guy!

Unfortunately, his mistakes were as epic as his successes. Not only did he sleep with his neighbor's wife, but he then had her husband killed to get him out of the way. He slaughtered whole armies, and his record of bloody war was the reason God prevented him from building the temple in Jerusalem. And, finally, he also fell victim to pride. Let's take a look at this story from the book of Samuel:

Then Satan stood against Israel and incited David to number Israel. So David said to Joab and the commanders of the army, "Go, number Israel, from

Beersheba to Dan, and bring me a report, that I may know their number." But Joab said, "May the LORD add to his people a hundred times as many as they are! Are they not, my lord the king, all of them my lord's servants? Why then should my lord require this? Why should it be a cause of guilt for Israel?" But the king's word prevailed against Joab.[4]

At first glance, this story seems innocent enough. After all, governments around the world conduct censuses regularly. Israel was supposed to live as God's chosen people, however, with their king humbly reliant upon God. In the ancient world there were only two reasons for a census: imposing new taxes or preparing for military campaigns. David's desire for a census meant he was planning to increase his royal power, dreaming about either increased revenue or a stronger military, things he himself could potentially put into motion, even if God hadn't called him to do so. This implied a lack of faith in God as the provider, with David taking charge of the nation's fate and seeking more than he had already been given. The story goes on to say that "God was displeased with this thing," and severe consequences followed.

We may not compete with King David's life for adventure, bloodshed, or intrigue, but we share his struggle with pride and self-reliance. How often have we imagined how much money we will make next year, or calculated what kind of house we might be able to afford someday? Or what about looking down, with a bit of smugness, upon those with less money or status than us? We have all probably been guilty of this throughout our lives. These small acts are our own version of King David's census. Just as God wanted Israel to humbly rely upon him, he desires the same from us.

A letter in the Bible was written to address this very point, about a thousand years after David's life had ended. It was written to the community of Jesus' followers in Laodicea, but it might as well have been penned to us today.

Laodicea, like many nations today, was prosperous and proud of it. Many citizens had plumbing, there was a town theater, and the marketplace teemed with activity. They had cutting-edge medical technology, and you could buy goods from Asia, Africa, or Italy, all without leaving town.[5] They took pride in how well-off they were, even refusing government assistance from Rome when recovering from a terrible earthquake, taking on a "we can do it ourselves" spirit.

But Jesus had strong words for the affluent church in Laodicea:

> I know your works: you are neither cold nor hot. Would that you were either cold or hot! So, because you are lukewarm, and neither hot nor cold, I will spit you out of my mouth. *For you say, I am rich, I have prospered, and I need nothing, not realizing that you are wretched, pitiable, poor, blind, and naked.* . . .

17

Those whom I love, I reprove and discipline, so be zealous and repent. Behold, I stand at the door and knock. If anyone hears my voice and opens the door, I will come in to him and eat with him, and he with me.[6]

This passage broke our hearts back in 2015 when we first realized Jesus was saying these words directly to us, MBA students with big plans for our future earnings. Thankfully, Jesus doesn't seek to condemn us. Rather, he patiently knocks, waiting for us to open the door so he can come in and eat with us. If we repent of our financially independent attitudes, we can enjoy the real riches of a deep relationship with him, gratefully depending on his provision as we live in faith.

We no longer depend on our own ability to earn money for sustenance in life. We work just as hard as we ever did, but now we recognize God as the provider, humbly thanking him for bringing resources to us. *Everything is a gift!* This mind-set fosters an amazing sense of peace. There's no need to obsess over counting our money or imagining what we'll earn next year when we instead recognize that God is the source of all good things and he loves us perfectly where we are today.

We imagine King David had a similar moment of conviction after the census. The aging king may have rolled back the tape in his mind's eye, saddened by his own pride, and remembered a special moment from his childhood.[7]

When someone praises you, do you directly accept the praise, or do you pass the credit along to God? Ascribing honor to God for our right deeds is an ancient Christian practice that builds gratitude. Next time someone praises you, try giving the credit to God!

"The prophet of God is here, and he's asked to see us!" Jesse shouted to his sons. "Boys, come quick!"

The prophet Samuel was a living legend throughout all Israel. The venerated leader carried almost unimaginable moral authority, and he spoke for God himself. Why was he here, in their little town, on their farm? The town leaders were terrified at first, but Samuel assured them he came in peace.

One by one, Samuel greeted the sons of Jesse. What an honor for them to meet this prophet of God! But Samuel seemed distracted. . . . Something was off. "Are all your sons here?" he asked.

Jesse told Samuel that his youngest, David, was far off in the fields watching sheep.

"Send for him!" Samuel demanded, impatiently waiting as one of the brothers scurried off to find David. (When the prophet asked for something, he got it.)

"David, come here!" his brother shouted, running out into the pasture where David was keeping the sheep. Winded from sprinting, he panted out, "The prophet . . . of God . . . wants to see you! Go!"

19

Leaving his brother with the sheep, David ran back, breathless, having missed all the commotion earlier. As he ran, he tried to figure out why he had been summoned. Was he in trouble? What was going on? He saw the crowd from a few hundred yards away and jogged up.

A broad, warm smile spread across Samuel's face when he saw David. "Come here, young man!"

Utterly confused and still catching his breath, David realized Samuel was now asking him to kneel. But why? Then Samuel began speaking about the anointing of God being upon David, and he poured a horn of oil over David's head. Through the oil dripping from his ears, David heard the words, ". . . anoint you as the future king of Israel."

We imagine David remembering this moment, smiling, tears welling up in his aging eyes. He had worked hard and applied himself at every stage of life, but it was undeniable that God had given him everything he had. A shepherd boy had become a great king.

Truly God is the One who raises men up and brings them down—the master of the nations. It's easy to get caught up in our accomplishments and our big plans, pridefully looking toward what else we can gain in the future. But as individuals who follow God, we must always remember the One who provides all that we have. And rather than lift our heads in pride, we can choose to take on postures of gratitude.

PRODIGALS

Bringing this theme of gratitude even closer to home, Jesus once told a story to show us who we are and who God is: the story of the prodigal son.[8] It's a story about faith, finances, and forgiveness.

A man had two sons. The younger asked for his inheritance early. This was a tremendous insult in Jewish society, perhaps equivalent today to a sixteen-year-old taking a bunch of money and leaving home with it, throwing up his middle finger at his father and yelling, "Wish you were dead! I'm never coming back!"

Jesus told us that the young man wasted the money on parties and prostitutes and hit rock bottom when the funds ran out. He got a job feeding pigs but was still going hungry. He finally hatched a desperate plan to return home and beg for a menial job as a hired hand. Jesus concluded the story,

> But while he was still a long way off, his father saw him and felt compassion, and ran and embraced him and kissed him. And the son said to him, "Father, I have sinned against heaven and before you. I am no longer worthy to be called your son." But the father said to his servants, "Bring quickly the best robe, and put it on him, and put a ring on his hand, and shoes on his feet. And bring the fattened calf and kill it, and let us eat and celebrate. For this my son was dead, and is alive again; he was lost, and is found." And they began to celebrate.[9]

Interestingly, the word *prodigal* actually means financially wasteful. The son failed morally and financially. The point of the story is that each of us has done the same. We are the prodigal; God is the Father. We have all sinned morally, rejecting the law of God. And none of us have saved, given, or spent our money perfectly. We are King David with his census; we are the Laodiceans with their independent spirits; we are the prodigal son with his reckless failures. This story shows that even if you're deeply in debt, even if you've run far from God, and even if you're wealthy and consumed with an ugly pride, God will still welcome you home with open arms if you'll come back to him.

Notice something here. The father was not taken off guard by the son's return. He didn't need a moment to figure out what to say. Instead, when the son was still a long way off, the father saw him coming back and *ran to meet him*. The father was watching the road! His patience and love were undiluted by the long wait, and his heart overflowed with welcoming love for his wayward son.

In the same way, in the midst of our failures, God watches the road for us to come home so he can embrace us with his love through the person and work of Jesus. His love is wild and astoundingly generous, and the value he places on us does not depend on our performance in the game of life. Whether or not you have credit card debt, whether or not you're a liar or a loser or full of lust, God wants to embrace you and put his best robe on your back, fresh sandals on your feet, and a ring on your finger. He wants you home, and Jesus made a way.

We can be as grateful as the prodigal son, based on the unmerited favor God has shown us.

A STORY OF HOPE

Our friend Chris experienced his own version of the prodigal son story, right here in the twenty-first century. He shared the following with us:

> Eighteen months ago, I blacked out on the streets of San Francisco on a Monday night. I came to under a bus stop, not knowing how I had gotten there, lost in the depths of an alcohol addiction several years old. I was drinking daily to the point where I couldn't feel anymore, barely able to keep life and work together. There wasn't much hope within me, just a growing amount of pain, guilt, and self-hatred.

To many who knew him from a distance, this was a surprise. Chris was exceptionally accomplished in life and a devoted follower of Jesus. He graduated with his MBA and had a great job paying six figures. He had even served in a leadership position at a college ministry and in various roles in his church. He explained that a performance-driven view of the world and his own faith caused him to buckle under the weight of life:

> Since [my] desire to do well and please others also translated into well-intentioned academic achievement and religious performance, I became used to . . . the

23

anxiety and fear it also nurtured, which ultimately fed the need to medicate with alcohol and other things to feel okay.

Thinking he had to earn his place as a Christian, or perform well enough to please God and others, life became too much to bear, and addiction began to take over. But then, the love of God came crashing in. Like David being anointed by Samuel, like the prodigal rejoicing in the father's gift of grace, Chris encountered God's abundant love in a brand-new way.

I'll never forget running into Chris at a business meeting and hearing him share, beaming with life, that God had reawakened in him a sense of awe, wonder, and confidence that his Father in heaven was pursuing him with a never-stopping love, even through the years of wandering. He was jubilant, having experienced God not as an angry judge but a loving Father waiting for him to come home. His life, and the things God asked him to steward, were not dependent on Chris doing everything right on his own. As he learned what it was to rest in the confidence of his Father's love, grateful for his sufficiency, he discovered a peace he never had before.

Chris recovered from his addiction, eventually leaving his Silicon Valley job to found OneStep, an online platform that connects individuals and families to inspirational, educational, and treatment resources around recovery and mental health. OneStep is structured to give the vast majority of profits away, in order that others can discover their God-given value and live lives of health and purpose through recovery. Any performance-driven pride Chris had before has been erased, and now his gratitude spills over in generosity. Chris said,

> I wake up each day pinching myself, knowing that I have been given not only another chance at life but also the opportunity to be fully alive in a way I didn't know was possible. When it becomes clear just how much each day of life is a gift, it becomes easier to give of time, life, and resource.

Chris's story is dramatic, but it illustrates what is at stake in every person's life. The most critical decision you will ever make is whether or not to recognize and respond to God's love for you, joyfully surrendering your life to his leading rather than continually trying to make everything happen on your own. Surrender goes hand in hand with salvation. When you accept the gift of salvation, your whole life comes under the authority and guidance of God, including your money.

Have you made the decision to follow Jesus and believe in his work for your eternal salvation? Visit truerichesbook.com/god to find out more.

If you haven't surrendered your life to Jesus, money management should be the least of your worries, and we'd encourage you to explore God deeply before getting too caught up in learning wise financial management. If you have surrendered your life to Jesus, *everything* can get rearranged by overwhelming gratitude, including how you think about and manage money.

Fundamentally, God wants our hearts. When he has our hearts, financially and otherwise, proper behaviors flow out naturally. Because of this, mechanical obedience to a rule is not what he's seeking, and it is totally inadequate to just take the normal financial wisdom of the world, slap on a tithe (10 percent giving), and assume that this constitutes Christian financial wisdom. God has far more of a joyful adventure in mind, an adventure that shapes not just what we do but what we become.

As Jesus said, "The good person out of the good treasure of his heart produces good, and the evil person out of his evil treasure produces evil."[10] We try to ask ourselves regularly, *What is deeply within my heart, underneath my financial behaviors?* If our hearts are full of gratitude for who God is and what he has given us, then we're poised to experience the joy of God with our money. If our hearts are full of pride at what we can experience or accomplish, we're on a road that tragically leads away from the true riches of life with God.

Moses explicitly pointed to this contrast of pride and gratitude, calling the people of Israel to remember God's goodness as the source of their increasing blessings. He advised, "Beware lest you say in your heart, 'My power and the might of my hand have gotten me this wealth.'

You shall remember the Lord your God, for it is he who gives you power to get wealth."[11]

Nearing the end of his life, David embraced Moses' advice, which he had surely read many times throughout his life, and came to a full appreciation of this truth.

KING DAVID'S GRATITUDE

God may not have allowed David to build the temple, but he did allow him to fund it. Remembering his own humble beginnings and God's central role in raising him up to greatness, David gave generously to set his son Solomon up for success in the temple-building project. He donated a fortune!

What do CEOs, kings, and billionaires typically talk about when they make the largest gift of their lives? They might reflect on their great journeys to wealth, talk about their visions for how the funds will be used, and craft each word to cement their own legacies. Or, if they're a bit shrewder, they might pump up their staff or subjects, talking about their shared greatness and building a culture of pride in the nation or company. Either way, it becomes clear that they are giving out of pride.

David took a radically different approach. The speech he gave in this moment of his great generosity has changed the lives of countless readers through the centuries for its powerful humility and gratitude. David would never make the mistake of the census again, and he gave us a model of the proper posture for giving. As you read his speech, pay attention to indications of gratitude.

Yours, O LORD, is the greatness and the power and the glory and the victory and the majesty, for all that is in the heavens and in the earth is yours. Yours is the kingdom, O LORD, and you are exalted as head above all. Both riches and honor come from you, and you rule over all. In your hand are power and might, and in your hand it is to make great and to give strength to all. And now we thank you, our God, and praise your glorious name.

But who am I, and what is my people, that we should be able thus to offer willingly? For all things come from you, and of your own have we given you. For we are strangers before you and sojourners, as all our fathers were. Our days on the earth are like a shadow, and there is no abiding.[12]

David knew God and gladly acknowledged that God alone raises up leaders, God alone gives wealth, God alone is eternal. Before him, our short lives are just a shadow. Our gifts are merely us giving back to God what was already his, but, in the process, he allows us to play on his team.

The prophet Jeremiah wrote, "Let not the rich man boast in his riches, but let him who boasts boast in this, that he understands and knows me, that I am the LORD who practices steadfast love, justice, and righteousness in the earth."[13] When we trade in our sense of self-importance for gratitude and begin partnering with God in his work, we discover the peace and fulfillment that has otherwise eluded us. Gratitude is the living thread that ties together the gospel, generosity, and God's grace in our hearts.

APPLICATION

We recommend "O Come to the Altar" by Elevation Worship as a great song to accompany this chapter's application exercise.

Fill in the table below to tally up your total gross income. (For some, income is so personal that even writing it down may be challenging. But we'll use this number later in the book to calculate savings rates and giving rates, so it's important to complete this first step in the process.)

MY TOTAL HOUSEHOLD INCOME

Source of Income	Explanation	Total Annual Income	Notes
Job #1	Gross income from first job (include salary and bonuses)		
Job #2	Gross income from second job (include salary and bonuses)		
Additional Income	Side gigs, pension, alimony, royalties, investment income, etc.		
Other Additional Income	Side gigs, pension, alimony, royalties, investment income, etc.		
TOTAL	Sum total of all rows.		

My Total Gross Family Income:_____

How does looking at your income make you feel? King Nebuchadnezzar, just before being punished by God for his pride, surveyed his income and his life and exclaimed, "Look at this, Babylon the great! I built it all by myself, a royal palace adequate to display my honor and glory!"[14]

Considering your income, reflect on these questions:

· Do I receive financial resources as a gift from God, or do I view them as the product of my own hard work, as Nebuchadnezzar did?
· Where am I on a spectrum from pride to gratitude?

Record your thoughts in your journal or below.

_____

_____

_____

_____

_____

_____

_____

_____

_____

_____

_____

_____

_____

_____

3

FROM COVETING TO CONTENTMENT

Keep your life free from the love of money, and be content with what you have, for he has said, "I will never leave you nor forsake you."

—*Hebrews 13:5*

We move from **Pride** to **Gratitude**
We move from **Coveting** to **Contentment**
We move from **Anxiety** to **Trust**
We move from **Indifference** to **Love**

SEVENTY MILLION DOLLARS.

My friend shared the number in a matter-of-fact way, like he was giving us the time of day. My wife, Megan, and I (John) were enjoying conversation with six Harvard MBA students in our Boston apartment in the fall of 2013. We had just finished a fun-filled Thanksgiving celebration, and most of our classmates had gone home. A few were lingering to watch the end of a football game, and our discussion had turned to the question of "how much is enough?" Would we ever stop seeking more money, power, and influence? Was there a point in life when it would be okay to stop pursuing more, smell the roses, and enjoy family and other pursuits? It was the smartest guy in the room who was first to reveal his target: $70 million.

We all had our own number, or at least a fuzzy idea of one. At the time my friend shared his number I remember thinking, *Gee. I must be a simple fellow. I'd be happy with a lot less.* But even though my number wasn't even close to $70 million, I still had one in mind. And the truth is, no matter what number we all had in mind, if we ever reached it, we'd likely still struggle to cease our efforts reaching for more. It's just the nature of this kind of thinking.

Do you have a number? If not a number, what about

a concept of "enough"? Is there a size of house that you would never go beyond, or a type of car that you would never upgrade from?

Contentment, in contrast to the endless striving reflected above, is a posture of the heart that rests peacefully in our present circumstances, no matter what they look like. It's a healing balm that helps us feel satisfied, rather than restless. But it can be hard to grasp, especially when we live in a culture driven so much by a consumer mentality.

THE ROOT CAUSE OF DEBT

Perhaps the most pervasive evidence of our lack of contentment is the consumer debt problem. In the most prosperous large economy in the history of the world, the United States in the twenty-first century, a large fraction of the population struggles to pay their bills and in fact falls further and further behind in their debts each month. How is this possible?

Perhaps the prevalence of consumer debt in our culture is merely the symptom of a deeper, hidden problem. Could there be a sin pattern that is so pervasive, so normalized, that we're blind to it, even as it consumes our lives and hinders our ability to connect with and serve God?

As a thought experiment, let's imagine a Christian community with rampant and public sexual sin. Imagine standing in the church lobby and hearing a church elder bragging about cheating on his wife. Confused, you turn aside, then overhear a friend talking about flirting and making sexual advances toward a coworker. Could this church be a faithful church while tolerating such brazen sin?

This example sounds ridiculous, but our wealthy society has cultivated just this kind of public and pervasive normalization of another sin: the sin of coveting. Some of us associate coveting with wanting someone else's stuff. Coveting isn't necessarily the desire to steal or take something from someone else, however. Coveting, at its core, is simply the belief that if I had more, I'd be happy. Think of it as striving, yearning, restlessly seeking more. It is a form of idolatry that leads us away from God.

You may not hear people brag about sexual sin in the church lobby, but we've probably all overheard small talk about the things we want to experience or buy. Being unhappy with our car and wanting a new one, chatting about so-and-so's new house and how nice it is (and maybe what they paid for it), or comparing vacation plans—any of these seemingly innocent topics can be neck-deep in covetousness.

It might be easy to criticize young students at Harvard Business School, daydreaming about whether their "number" is $10 million or $70 million and debating the pros and cons of owning a private jet. However, when we experience envy over a friend's kitchen remodel or a jealous twinge at the thought of someone else getting the newest smartphone, we're guilty of the same sin. Whether we're chasing millions of dollars or just another day's wages, each of our human hearts is prone to covet what others have, to continually be looking for more than we're given.

Here's something fascinating you might see, though, as you study the Bible. That sinful desire for more that leads our hearts away from God—it's present both when we covet material blessings and when we sin sexually. In fact, sexual sin and coveting are linked together throughout the Bible. Both sins are prohibited in the original Ten Commandments. And the apostle Paul wrote, "For you may be sure of this, that everyone who is sexually immoral or impure, or who is covetous (that is, an idolater), has no inheritance in the kingdom of Christ and God."[1]

The book of Hebrews features a pair of commands in immediate succession related to sex and money:

> Let marriage be held in honor among all, and let the marriage bed be undefiled, for God will judge the sexually immoral and adulterous. Keep your life free from the love of money, and be content with what you have, for he has said, "I will never leave you nor forsake you."[2]

It's easy for us to agree that unrepentant, flagrant sexual sin indicates a lack of true faith or devotion to Jesus. But the Bible says the same is true for unrepentant, flagrant coveting. Both involve disregarding healthy boundaries and limits in our individual human lives. Indeed, Ambrose of Milan wrote over 1,600 years ago that "the only difference between [a greedy man] and an adulterer is that one has an inordinate love for physical form, the other, a desire for a farm, a rich estate."[3]

God gives us healthy boundaries in our finances and in our sexual purity. Violating these boundaries by pursuing ungodly sexual fulfillment, or by spending too much, is a rejection of God's good plan for human flourishing. Bible scholar N. T. Wright, reflecting on the distinctiveness of the early Jesus communities in the first century, noted that "Sexual purity and financial generosity were to be built into the Christian DNA from the start."[4]

Thus, sex and money are not side topics for God's people, areas of life we can submit to Jesus when we get around to them. They are central issues for the ethic of Christ and his church. Our culture teaches us to be generous with sex and to closely guard our money. But God teaches us to be generous with money and to closely guard our sexual purity. It's a total reversal—one that leads us, in both cases, toward a divine contentment that wisely stewards what God has given us!

If you're reading this in a climate-controlled room and know where your next meal is going to come from, you're among the huge number of people who have been given amazing prosperity here in the twenty-first century. We tend to take for granted our access to food and drink, a soft bed, and plenty of clothing. Yet even in the midst of this abundance, we've been seduced by the pursuit of a nicer lifestyle and find ourselves struggling to give even 10 percent of our income away. The church collectively prayed, "Give us this day our daily bread," and God answered the prayer, generously entrusting us with enough funds to buy *mountains* of bread. Instead of sharing it where he intended, however, we ate our fill and then used what was left to get nicer homes, cars, vacations, and private schools, until there was nothing left to share.

According to Hebrews, this sin is in the same category as living a life of unrestrained sexual promiscuity. Let's say that again. *Spending all of our income on ourselves in pursuit of fulfillment, to the detriment of our generosity, is like regularly committing adultery.* What has led us so far astray from God's vision of joyful contentment? Let's face it. We are coveters, and we live in a society where coveting is normalized. Like the frog in the pot that never notices the water is boiling until it's too late, we're surrounded with a dangerous environment. We need someone outside the pot to help us. Thankfully, our God is ready to help and has provided a path of escape.

God invites us to a greater joy—a path away from the treadmill of coveting. As my pastor said, "There are two ways to be rich. One is to have a lot of money, and the other is to just not need a lot of money." This chapter is about God's invitation toward becoming rich the second way, through the joy of contentment.

OUR PERSONAL CONTENTMENT JOURNEYS

As we've navigated life and built families with our wives, we've had to make the ubiquitous choices. Where do we live? What cars do we buy? Should we eat out tonight? We constantly make mistakes and are always learning, but we're grateful for how much God has taught us along the way.

Our lifestyle ambitions were sky-high before and during our time at Harvard, until God flipped our perspective,

37

challenging us to live with contentment rather than covetousness. At graduation, I (Greg) planned on buying an Acura to celebrate and to gain a reliable luxury vehicle that would last for years. I could afford it, no question. But Alison, my wife, challenged me.

"Do you really need a car that nice?" She spoke with God's voice (as she usually does), and it caused me to consider the call of contentment. Eventually, instead of buying that Acura, I happily took over my grandmother's thirteen-year-old Mercury Grand Marquis. I love my old granny car, because it reminds me continually that my value is in Christ, not in my stuff. I saved a lot of money on a car purchase. Far more important than that, however, is that my old, uncool car trains my heart.

In the parable of the sower, Jesus taught that chasing a fancy lifestyle makes us like a plant trying to grow up inside a thorn bush—unproductive and choked out. "As for what was sown among thorns, this is the one who hears the word, but the cares of the world and the deceitfulness of riches choke the word, and it proves unfruitful."[5] We've both seen this choking effect in our own lives whenever we start to drift toward coveting, rather than contentment.

I (John) used to drive past multimillion-dollar homes and feel my stomach turn. We owned a nice home we could pay off within ten to fifteen years without impeding our generosity, but I felt an anxiety, a striving, a relentless pull to obtain something better for my family. Proverbs 14:30 says that "envy makes the bones rot," and mine were rotting. If it was possible for some other guy's family to live like that, in a huge house on the lake, then it should be possible for mine too! As God taught me his view of money and possessions, this gripping sense of striving began to fade.

I will never own a large estate home or a home in the best neighborhood in town, and I'm entirely at peace with that knowledge. When I drive past one, I think, *Wow, what a beautiful home! I'm not pursuing a house like that, and I'm perfectly okay.* Instead of striving and jealousy, I feel peace and joy within my own circumstances. Jesus taught that "one's life does not consist in the abundance of his possessions,"[6] and he has helped me discover an abundant life based on more than what I own.

Basil of Caesarea discerningly observed that, "When wealth is divided by a man and a woman between so many pursuits, and each vies to outdo the other in the invention of frivolous amusements, there is of course no opportunity to consider the needs of others."[7] He nailed us! But the converse is also true: when people set out to discover joyful simplicity, there is more room to give and share with others.

God has given us tremendous grace as he's taught us contentment. To be clear, contentment does not mean "pious frugality"—depriving ourselves of all spending, all the time. Both our families enjoy nice lifestyles. But it does mean embracing relative simplicity and choosing to thank God for what he has already given us. Pastor Jon Tyson calls this a "provocative lifestyle distinction" by which Christians live significantly more modest lives than their peers because of their dedication to the gospel. And by living simply, more money is available for giving!

We're so grateful for God's invitation to discover his way of thinking about lifestyle, and that he has shown us how to enjoy daily life without being consumed by the endless desire for more.

YOU CAN'T TAKE IT WITH YOU

As we have spent less and embraced contentment, we've paradoxically experienced gain. Life is better when we let go of coveting and stop striving after more. Paul shared this same view with his young pastor friend Timothy:

> Godliness with contentment is great gain, for we brought nothing into the world, and we cannot take anything out of the world. But if we have food and clothing, with these we will be content. But those who desire to be rich fall into temptation, into a snare, into many senseless and harmful desires that plunge people into ruin and destruction. For the love of money is a root of all kinds of evils. It is through this craving that some have wandered away from the faith and pierced themselves with many pangs.[8]

Paul is going directly against our American ethos here. The desire to be rich is senseless, harmful, and a root of many evils—wow! Paul worked hard in a respectable profession as a tentmaker and elsewhere encouraged people to provide for their families.[9] He clearly wasn't antiwork. He was just antidistraction. He was reinforcing Jesus' perspective that life is about more than money and possessions

40

and that the things we covet make empty promises. They can't fulfill us. As a friend said recently, "I finally bought the car I'd been wanting, and to my surprise I suddenly felt fear and restriction, not freedom and joy."

The acquisitive desire for riches, fueled by coveting, dominated Egypt during the time the people of Israel were enslaved there. God delivered them from this system in the exodus, just as he wants to deliver you and me. Pharaoh's world was a world of scarcity and a world of taking. If you didn't take food, labor, and wealth from others, it would be taken from you. The strong ruled, and the weak served. God brought Israel out of Pharaoh's economy and into his own economy of abundance. Manna—bread from heaven—was available every day. There was to be equality, sharing, community, and love. The strong were to care for the weak, and all were to welcome the foreigner. There was even a day for *not working*, the Sabbath, a day to break the power of coveting over the human heart.

As theologian Walter Brueggemann said, "If we trace . . . from Adam to Moses we may suggest that the core story is a story about coveting."[10] But God came to break through that core story, teaching his people that he alone was their sufficiency and that having more stuff would never bring fulfillment. Unfortunately, we too often try to leave the promised land and head back into Egypt, chaining ourselves to the endless pursuit after more.

Indeed, the ancient book of Ecclesiastes spends a good deal of time deconstructing the pursuit of wealth and possessions, demonstrating how frivolous it is. The author noted that "whoever loves money never has enough; whoever loves wealth is never satisfied with their income. This too is meaningless."[11] Chasing money or possessions for their own sake is a tragic way to spend our time.

No one wishes from their deathbed that they had built more wealth or bought a bigger house. They wish they had spent more time with their family, or that they had lived a life with more meaning. A friend recently summed this up well after her elderly parents died: "I spent all day yesterday clearing out my parents' stuff from their house. Why do we hold on to all these possessions so tightly? Why did they have all this *stuff*? The pieces go back in the box when the game is over."

When Paul wrote about godliness and contentment, it was more than empty theory. He had lived it. You know that famous Bible verse, "I can do all things through him who strengthens me"? This is often the go-to verse for athletes competing in sporting events. It has inspired countless young people to work harder to perfect their skills, but is that what the verse was really intended for?

Almost everyone has heard this verse, but fewer people know that Paul wrote it about money and lifestyle. He didn't write those famous words after winning a game; he wrote them from prison, after receiving a large financial gift.

I have learned in whatever situation I am to be content. I know how to be brought low, and I know how to abound. In any and every circumstance, I have learned the secret of facing plenty and hunger, abundance and need. I can do all things through him who strengthens me.[12]

When the Philippian church heard of Paul's imprisonment, they'd sent a messenger on a long, risky journey to bring him a generous gift of provision. It may have included a warm coat for cold nights, along with funds to improve his meager prisoner's diet. Paul wrote these words to let them know of his great gratitude. But he also wanted them to know that his joy was already secure before the gift, that joy in Christ is not dependent on circumstances.

Paul had been hungry, shipwrecked, beaten with rods, whipped, imprisoned, and he had shivered through cold nights from exposure. He had also dined with elites, enjoyed the benefits of prestigious Roman citizenship, and received an Ivy League–level education.[13] He knew how to be joyfully rich and how to be joyfully poor. The secret of both is simply Christ. He knew that contentment is a state of mind in Christ, not a state of affairs in the world.

JOYFUL CONTENTMENT IN SUFFERING

Paul learned his contentment from Jesus, as millions of Christians have since. Suffering and being in want, whether that means financially or otherwise, characterized Jesus' life and were common for his early followers. In spite of this trend, Christians practiced joyful contentment as a hallmark of their faith. As Wess Stafford, president emeritus of Compassion International, put it: "Joy is a decision, a very brave one, about how you are going to *respond* to life."[14]

In fact, our joyful contentment can produce a ripple effect. The church in Thessalonica "received the word in much affliction, and with the joy of the Holy Spirit," according to Paul's correspondence. He told them, "You became an example to all the believers in Macedonia."[15] The Thessalonians could have chosen to sit in their suffering, in their lack, and wish for a different reality, as we all sometimes do. Instead, they embraced the joy of the Holy Spirit, and the news of their joyful contentment reached even as far as the church in Macedonia.

Five years later, Paul described what the Macedonians did with what they had picked up from the church in Thessalonica: "In a severe test of affliction, their abundance of joy and their extreme poverty have overflowed in a wealth of generosity" toward the Christians in Jerusalem in their time of need.[16]

Notice the chain reaction of impact!

1. The Thessalonians faithfully chose joy in hardship and lack.
2. The Macedonians learned from it and mimicked this Christlike joy in suffering.
3. This joy enabled the Macedonians, despite their poverty, to give generously.
4. This generosity met the needs of the Christians in Jerusalem.
5. Their story inspires us to give today.
6. Our generosity blesses and inspires others.
7. And so on!

Imagine a scene in heaven: a man from Jerusalem, who became a Christian when influenced by the church there, finds a woman from Thessalonica, who suffered with patience and joy.

"You never knew this," he says, "but your joyful contentment in hardship led to a chain reaction of events that eventually included my own salvation. Thank you!"

She begins to feel overwhelmed with gratitude, but he continues, "My extended family has planned a party for you. There are a hundred thousand people here in heaven from among my descendants, stretching across fifty generations, who all know the Lord because of my conversion, which resulted from your faithful obedience."

The woman may have lived a humble life and never imagined that anyone really noticed her. This moment would be one of her greatest rewards. Our faithful joy and contented spirit produce a ripple effect, the results of which we may never fully know. We look for results and influence here and now, but God is moving across nations and generations.

Many of us may face jobs we don't like, extended unemployment, the loss of a loved one, or a debilitating sickness. Bad circumstances are universal. It has been said that everyone is coming out of a crisis, is in crisis, or is about to enter a crisis, and we would trade these hardships for less-painful situations if we could. But as followers of Jesus we are called to put away all forms of covetousness, so when these times come we must ask ourselves, how will we respond? If our value and identity and trust is placed in our Father God, we can respond with joyful contentment. We're playing a long game and know that our present circumstances are very temporary in light of eternity. We're confident that someday we'll enter into the fullness of God's presence, and that our seasons of lack will be wiped away. This perspective can transform our suffering into something incredibly powerful: a witness to the goodness of God even in bad circumstances.

An American pastor visited a country overseas that is experiencing explosive growth in their Christian population. He said, "They have a fivefold plan to grow the church. Every day, each Christian should read the Bible, pray, talk about Jesus with someone, and expect a miracle. Those are the first four, and they're amazing. But the fifth goal is different: *develop a theology of suffering.* They told me that God can move more powerfully through the sufferings of his people than through their comforts, and they want to be ready to suffer well, for the glory of God."[17]

This is a way of thinking that is so counter to our culture that continually seeks more comfort, more provision, and less hardship. It's something that can be hard to wrap our minds around, and yet maybe they're on to something. Rather than driving toward more security and comfort, they live simply, preparing their hearts for the struggles ahead. Indeed, another one of our friends soon relayed an amazing story that demonstrated this principle in action.

HOPE IN THE DARKNESS

Sitting cross-legged on the dirt floor, halfway around the world, our friend ate a skimpy bowl of gruel that his hosts had given him. They wore facial coverings, so he could only hear their voices. "Aren't you going to eat?" he asked them.

"No. We are fasting. Our ordeal begins next month."

His hosts were Christians who had snuck out of their oppressive, anti-Christian nation to seek spiritual and theological training. He was visiting them for only one day and had just joined them at their secretive, rural retreat.

"What do you mean by 'ordeal'?"

"We want to go back home to teach and train our brothers and sisters in Christ. When we return, our extended absence from the country without a visa will get us in trouble, and we'll be punished. We will be imprisoned and will be beaten, tortured, and interrogated. This will last for months or years. Afterward they will let us go, and we can go minister. Eventually, if we are ever discovered, we will be executed. Only then will we have rest—eternal rest in Jesus."

Even their veils, his host later explained, were worn in preparation for what was to come. Each person wore them to protect one another's anonymity so that later, under torture, they would not crack and identify fellow participants in the training. Despite the somber circumstances, however, these pastors-in-training were peaceful, resolute, and calm. Not only were they financially poor, they were also facing the threat of imminent torture and death.

Our friend later recounted this visit with these brave individuals. "They talk about baptism differently than we do. We talk about being baptized into new life. That's true and beautiful. But we forget about the dying part. Baptism symbolizes the death of the old self.[18] Death to our own plans. Death to comfort and security, if these things stand in the way of discipleship. These friends spoke of being 'baptized into the death of Jesus,' and they knew that it might literally mean their own death at the hands of oppressors."

His eyes welled with tears as he continued. "They'll never be beatified as saints by the Catholic church. Won't ever get invited to speak at Protestant megachurches. They're anonymous, and no earthly fame will ever come their way. But I'm not even worthy to sit at their feet. We need their perspective, their wisdom, their devotion. We have so much to learn from them."

As he shared, I (John) quickly felt humbled to my core. I want to learn how to have the contented peace of these persecuted leaders. I want to lean on Jesus as hard as they do! I may not be called to imprisonment for Jesus, but I do have the opportunity to stretch my giving beyond 15 percent of my gross income. That kind of stretching tends to make me worry about things like getting my house paid off quickly enough or being able to take the kinds of vacations I'd like, but perhaps that's just my own small way of growing into the generous contentment that Jesus calls us all toward. Martyrdom is the ultimate act of generosity—to literally give up your life for God. I may not become a true martyr, but I can be a living sacrifice, generous in my giving and joyfully content in every circumstance of my life.

Dietrich Bonhoeffer suffered and eventually died at the hands of the Nazis, yet he faithfully proclaimed the gospel until the end. He wrote about our cheapening of the Christian faith: how it has become something nice to believe, and a good set of morals, and a source of comfort for when we die. He bemoaned our loss of the sense that a choice to follow Jesus is all or nothing, requiring action in our life and in our finances too. He wrote,

> Jesus says that every Christian has his own cross waiting for him, a cross destined and appointed by God. Each must endure his allotted share of suffering and rejection. But each has a different share: some God deems worthy of the highest form of suffering, and gives them the grace of martyrdom, while others he does not allow to be tempted above that which they are able to bear. But it is the one and the same cross in every case.[19]

Jesus calls us to follow, and sometimes his call means losing our lives, losing our families, or being kicked out of our professions. Sometimes it means something less extreme: a call to raise godly families, disciple other believers, and to live simple, contented lives marked by generosity rather than covetousness. Most of us can be thankful that we haven't been asked to undergo torture and physical suffering for our profession of the gospel. But we do have a challenging and liberating task: the everyday commitment to silence the voice of coveting so that we can live simply, work diligently, and give generously.

GRACE, NOT GUILT

Let's pause here for a moment to clarify one point. So often when Christian teaching touches on the issues we're discussing, guilt, shame, and duty take over. We zone out, shut down, and move on. When we see a moral requirement that looks painful and feels awkward, we just skip the page, tune out the sermon, or exit the conversation.

Our invitation from God, however, is to a joyful relationship driven by gratitude, contentment, trust, and love. Not obedience to a law. Not a guilt trip into a lifestyle change. Rather, he invites us into exuberant and abundant life.

Tuition in Jesus' school of discipleship is set on a sliding scale—the price of admission is everything you have. But if you enroll, you gain everything the God of the universe has to offer, including eternal life. The high cost of following Jesus is acceptable only if we believe in the reward. Profit is what you gain minus what you invest. You've got to invest it all, but your reward is far bigger than you can imagine.

God says, "Give me everything—all that you are. And I'll give you everything—all that I am."

Some people hesitate or walk away because the cost is too high. Their view of their own lives is too lofty, or their view of God is too diminished. One young man met Jesus and went away sad at what it would cost to follow.[20] But others gladly jump in, because the reward is so big.[21] Jesus knew this would happen, and he told stories to illustrate the high cost mixed with the joy of discovery:

"Again, the kingdom of heaven is like a merchant in search of fine pearls, who, on finding one pearl of great value, went and sold all that he had and bought it."[22]

A modern rendition might be: The kingdom of heaven is like a property investor who, upon finding the deal of a lifetime, joyfully sold all that he had to buy it.

Jesus is the greatest discovery you can ever make in your life. He's the treasure you've been seeking. He's the deal of a lifetime. You might imagine that the price tag to gain his tutelage is far too expensive. Remarkably, he doesn't require you to have $1 million, or a pretty good track record of behavior, or a picture-perfect family. He just says, "Bring all that you have. I want it all, and it's perfectly enough."

TWO KEYS TO CONTENTMENT

Following Jesus out of the trap of always wanting more, of covetousness, leads us to the richness of a contentment that enables generosity. But what does this look like in practice? Let's consider a few ideas that help us get past the constant ache for more and experience financial peace with God. The first is *margin*, for those of us with limited incomes, and the second is *enough*, for those of us with high incomes.

Margin

Creating margin in your life means making sure you have extra money every single month. Margin happens when you spend less than you earn. We consider margin to be the number-one principle for successful money management, because without it you cannot consistently give or save.

If we want to save and give in a meaningful way, though, we need to do far better than just spending a little bit less than we earn. We need to spend *way* less than we earn! Let's say you pay 15 percent in taxes and have a goal to give 15 percent and save 15 percent.

In this back-of-the-envelope example, that leaves just 55 percent for spending! This takes some careful accounting and planning to pull off well.

Total Income	100%
Taxes	-15%
Savings	-15%
Giving	-15%
Left for Spending	55%

Margin is God's gift to people with limited incomes: a way to plan for the future and to plan for generosity even when we're not wealthy. Indeed, God *commanded* poor Israelite farmers to maintain margin so that they could be givers.

> When you reap the harvest of your land, you shall not reap your field right up to its edge, neither shall you gather the gleanings after your harvest. And you shall not strip your vineyard bare, neither shall you gather the fallen grapes of your vineyard. You shall leave them for the poor and the sojourner: I am the LORD your God.[23]

Back then, agricultural output was essentially equivalent to money. An efficient, diligent farmer would want to get every last grape! So it was a sacrifice, an intentional practice in contentment and generosity, to follow God's command. If this passage were written today it would say something like, "Keep margin in your finances. Don't spend every dollar, but instead leave money free so you have some available for giving to the poor."

When we're living maxed out, spending all that we earn, the idea of spending less is uncomfortable. Sometimes the only way to generate margin is to embrace major lifestyle changes. But margin is the only path to financial health and to Christian faithfulness. Better yet, it's the financial path to peace and joy. If you find yourself struggling with this idea, pause now and pray. Christ can give you the strength you need to take action in pursuit of margin in your life. We'll explore tangible steps you can take in the application section of this chapter.

Consider setting up a special savings account with a few hundred dollars in it for spontaneous giving. Then, if you see a need and God prompts you to give, you can freely and immediately act, knowing you have the money already set aside for generosity.

Enough

If God provides someone with a high income, it becomes critically important to figure out what "enough" looks like. A Christian who is biblically content and striving toward generosity will not seek to continually ramp up his or her lifestyle. When we discover the value of God and his kingdom, our desires move from ramping up our lifestyle toward ramping up our contribution to God's work.

There is nothing wrong with aspiring for a better job, seeking stable housing, or hoping for a reliable car. It's perfectly okay to have nice things and enjoy them as the blessings of God. You may live a nicer life at age forty than you did as a college student. However, Jesus warned against the dangers of the continual pursuit of more with no limits.

Many of the families we admire in financial discipleship have settled on the notion of "enough" in their lifestyle. They know where the line is drawn for them and have stopped worrying about the acquisition of more toys, experiences, or square footage. For some of them, "enough" looks like this:

- A couple owns a billion-dollar company and has many children. They take a salary of $140,000 per year, live in a modest home, and give away tens of millions of dollars per year.
- A family who can afford a prestigious private school instead sends their children to a less expensive, co-op school as an act of faithful stewardship, so they can give the difference away.
- A young entrepreneur starts a company with nothing, and he and his wife scrape by and diligently pay off debts. When the business succeeds and their income hits $1 million per year, they still choose to live simply in a modest four-bedroom home and give generously.

The point of setting a limit is not to achieve right-eousness by enacting some random rule or to enable us to cast judgment on others who spend more than we do. In fact, a poverty mind-set is sinful as well. The Old Testament commands many feasts and celebrations, and Jesus feasted with his disciples. A well-timed vacation or a beautifully decorated living room can be delightful and worth celebrating. It's easy for many people, including us, to become overly harsh toward our spouses or other close friends, criticizing the smallest of spending mistakes. That doesn't make us wise or frugal. It just makes us jerks!

Thus, the balance we're after here is joyful, grace-filled simplicity. If you have a high income, would it be wise to make your family of five live in an old studio apartment so you can give more of your income away? Probably not. But we've never met anyone who has done that. In our culture we usually don't need protection from underspending; we need a guardrail to protect us against lifestyle creep. Remember, Jesus warned that some of his potential followers would be thwarted by the "cares of the world and the deceitfulness of riches," making their lives "unfruitful."[24]

Cars provide a very useful illustration. There were no cars in Jesus' day, but he did ride into Jerusalem on a donkey, the transportation method of the simple and the poor. This indicated he was a king coming in peace and simplicity, rather than with the wartime grandeur of a stallion or chariot. A lowly donkey was good enough for our Christ. This begs the question: In an age where financially successful people drive luxury automobiles, should Christians follow suit, or should we follow the example of our Lord, choosing simplicity and humility in our transportation?

We know a Christian CEO who, for many years, drove a beat-up old car whose speedometer functioned only sporadically. And another who always buys used cars and refuses to spend more than $15,000 on one. And an internationally known ministry leader who drives a modest, high-mileage Toyota Camry. None of these people are experiencing lack, but they've all rejected the car-status game in order to focus their time, attention, and affections on things of greater importance and value. Our choice of car is a fantastic opportunity to model the simple humility of Jesus.

In cars and in all of life, we propose that we all stop asking, "How much do I need to give?" and instead start asking, "How much do I really need to keep?" For us, personally, our families have decided that we won't spend more than $100,000 per year, no matter what kind of income we may earn, freeing up any excess beyond that figure to be invested back into God's kingdom.[25] To be clear, $100,000 affords a very nice lifestyle; again, biblical stewardship is not simply a thriftiness contest. We settled on $100,000 because this figure allows us to provide a nice lifestyle for our families without seeping into luxury simply for luxury's sake. Other families will arrive at different numbers, and we challenge all families to take the time to consider what number makes sense for them.[26] Whether that number is $50,000, $150,000, or something else, the point is to wrestle with the question so many of us struggle to answer: "How much is 'enough'?"

In total, John currently earns $150,000 to $200,000 per year.[27] After taxes, diligent saving, and giving, about $80,000 remains for spending each year—not the full $100,000 that would theoretically be a maximum based on his family's finish-line commitment. Thus, his family hasn't reached their spending finish line but is content with their current lifestyle nonetheless. Greg currently earns significantly more and could spend above his finish-line amount while still saving and giving a lot. Despite this ability to spend, his family has chosen to limit their spending to the $100,000 finish line, in recognition that God has provided more than enough for their thriving and the extra is for God's kingdom.

Drawing a line on lifestyle can ensure fruitfulness. It's not a mandate from Scripture, but it's a best practice that we've implemented in our lives in our pursuit of true riches. Ultimately, life is about more than spending money, and our spending should *always* face a constraint, as indicated in the chart below:

My Income Is . . .	My Spending Should Be Limited By . . .
Modest	The need for *margin*, so that I have financial breathing room
High	The need to recognize *enough*, so that I avoid becoming distracted and unfruitful

If we are not affluent, our spending will be constrained by the need for margin. We'll avoid spending all our income, because we want to leave room for saving and giving. If we achieve relative affluence, however, it becomes possible to ramp up our lifestyles toward increasing comfort, even while maintaining healthy margin. This feels like a blessing, but it is also a remarkably deceptive and dangerous game. Without a healthy concept of "enough" we run the risk of being choked out in our fruitfulness as Christians by the pursuit of toys, distractions, and luxuries. Luxuries aren't necessarily bad, but for Christians they are a risky distraction and are best thought of as the exception rather than the rule.

As the Cortines family began to experience a new level of financial income entering 2017, we set a goal to increase our margin and live with "enough." We wanted to give away $20,000. It was a scary, faith-filled number for us. But at year-end, when we added up the numbers, we had given away $36,494! That represented 23 percent of our total gross income. Somehow, our finances were healthier than they had ever been even after all that giving. Our lifestyle hadn't changed, God had brought increase, and our giving was taken to new heights as God opened doors of opportunity. It was amazing! We would have loved a new car, and God would not have loved us any less if we bought one. But we were overjoyed to have given those funds away while practicing a contented, stable lifestyle.

When our income is lower, we limit our spending to achieve *margin*. When our income is higher, we limit our spending to honor the principle of *enough*. These two principles will help us follow Christ's plan for contentment in our lives and will slowly but surely help us break free from habits of coveting.

APPLICATION

We recommend "Even When It Hurts" by Hillsong United as a great song to accompany this chapter's application exercise.

Answer the following two questions, reflecting on your journey of contentment in spending.

Do I have margin in my financial life, in obedience to Leviticus 19?
  a. Absolutely—Every month I'm able to save and give a significant fraction of my income (i.e., a surprise $500 expense is not an emergency; I'll just pay for it out of cashflow).
  b. Maybe—Some months might be closer to break-even, but I save and give most months.
  c. Not Really—I am month-to-month in my cashflow and don't save or give much.

Do I have a clear picture of "enough," ensuring I avoid the fate of the third soil in Matthew 13?
  a. Absolutely—I know the maximum lifestyle I would be comfortable living, and I've committed to others to stay faithful to this vision.
  b. Maybe—I want to avoid lifestyle creep but am not too sure what that looks like.
  c. Not Really—I aspire to ramp up my lifestyle as my income allows. I've never really thought about or considered limiting my expenditures.

What do you notice in your answers? Write down any reflections in your journal or in the space below.

_____

_____

_____

_____

_____

_____

Creating margin and embracing "enough" may mean radical changes—changes that are both difficult and worthwhile. Often, when we think of spending less, we think of eating out less or clipping grocery coupons. In reality, though, it is often the big-ticket items in life that dominate a family budget. Without reengineering these budgetary drivers, real and lasting change proves elusive.

In other words, resisting your urge to splurge on Chick-fil-A is not going to change the game if your mortgage is three times your income and you drive a luxury car or shiny new truck or SUV. You can enjoy that chicken sandwich without guilt, but tough love says you may need to downsize the house or trade in the expensive car for a reliable, used sedan. To be clear, it's not always wrong to spend a lot on homes or cars. But it is definitely wrong sometimes. Careful consideration is needed.

Randy Alcorn wrote,

Today, there are . . . two kinds of disciples—one who gives up his income and possessions to further the cause in full-time ministry, and one who earns an income to generously support the same cause. (We should be careful not to discourage one another from either of these callings.)

There is not, however, a third kind of disciple, who does whatever he or she feels like with money and possessions and fails to use them for the kingdom. Such people are common today, but by New Testament standards they are not disciples.[28]

For the below "big four" budgetary items, evaluate where you stand in terms of keeping margin and understanding "enough." Fill in the table below or jot down your answers in your own journal.

Big-Ticket Item	Margin Test Put a check mark if this item is easily affordable, or a question mark if it stretches your budget.	"Enough" Test Put a check mark if you have a clear picture of "enough" in this area, or a question mark if you're inclined to strive for more when your income allows it.
House(s)		
Car(s)		
Trips/ Vacations		
Education		

Circle and take note of any question marks in the previous table. Is there one key action step that emerges from this reflection? What change, if any, might be needed? What should you commit to prayer?

Write the answers below or in your journal.

_____

_____

_____

_____

_____

_____

_____

_____

_____

_____

_____

_____

_____

_____

_____

_____

_____

_____

_____

_____

_____

4

FROM ANXIETY
TO TRUST

Therefore do not be anxious, saying, "What shall we eat?" or "What shall we drink?" or "What shall we wear?" . . . But seek first the kingdom of God and his righteousness, and all these things will be added to you.

—Jesus, Matthew 6:31, 33

We move from **Pride** to **Gratitude**
We move from **Coveting** to **Contentment**
We move from **Anxiety** to **Trust**
We move from **Indifference** to **Love**

IMAGINE LOGGING INTO your online bank account one Friday expecting to see your latest paycheck deposit but instead finding that your account balance is $0.00. Z-e-r-o. Zilch. What emotions would you feel in that moment?

Obviously losing *all* your money would be anxiety-provoking. Even losing *a little* money, however, causes significant stress for many people. Most would avoid the risk of losing one hundred dollars even if doing so meant forfeiting an equal or even greater chance of winning one hundred dollars. Psychologists call this *loss aversion*.[1] Loss aversion is driven by humans' fear of the unknown. This fear, this anxiety about future what-if scenarios, compels us to stockpile what we have now *just in case*. Proverbs 21:20 says that "precious treasure and oil are in a wise man's dwelling, but a foolish man devours it." Consistent, responsible saving is certainly core to faithful financial planning. However, when taken too far, saving money can become a crutch—something we lean on too much due to our anxiety about the future.

This is a common temptation. Money is among the leading causes of stress for most Americans.[2] Why do we suffer so much anxiety? Likely because we lack trust—trust in God's promises and in his provision.

Jesus said, "Therefore do not be anxious, saying, 'What shall we eat?' or 'What shall we drink?' or 'What shall we wear?' . . . But seek first the kingdom of God and his righteousness, and all these things will be added to you."[3] In Luke 12, a parallel passage to Matthew 6, Jesus said, "Fear not, little flock, for it is your Father's good pleasure to give you the kingdom."[4] If we believe we have a good Father and that everything Jesus taught is true, our response when anxiety and fear bubble up in our hearts should be one of trust as we remember who holds the future. Learning to trust God enables us to find authentic security and satisfaction in our true provider, opening the door to the incredible, unmatched joy he offers to those who choose to live not only fearlessly but generously.

IDOLATRY AND ANXIETY

While anxiety about money is endemic in our modern society, it is certainly nothing new. The Bible tells the story of a wealthy, young ruler who approached Jesus to ask what he must do to "inherit eternal life" (Luke 18:18). The ruler clarified that he had obediently kept all God's commandments "from [his] youth." Jesus replied, "One thing you still lack. Sell all that you have and distribute to the poor, and you will have treasure in heaven." When the ruler heard these words, "he became very sad, for he was extremely rich."[5]

Jesus calls all his followers to open-handed generosity, but this is the only place in Scripture where he specifically told someone to give away *everything he owned*. In fact, in the very next chapter of Luke, Jesus announced that "today salvation has come to this house" when the corrupt tax collector Zacchaeus repented and gave away *half* of his possessions.[6] The rich young ruler attempted to find meaning and security in his possessions. So Christ's specific call on his life was to give up those possessions, which were preventing him from fully trusting in God.

Don't we all suffer to some extent from the same challenges faced by the young ruler? We attend church on Sundays, say our bedtime prayers, maybe give away a fraction of our income, all while constantly fretting over our finances—either by stressing over our bills or savings, or by vainly attaching our security and self-worth to our possessions and wealth.

I (Greg) succumb to the temptation to seek (false) security in money all the time. I allow myself to believe that having just a little more money would abate the anxiety and insecurity I feel about my future. I've been tempted to feel this way when I had negative wealth (thank you, student loans), and again after I became a homeowner, and even still as my retirement accounts get larger and larger as my career progresses. Having more hasn't solved the anxiety. If anything, it can make it worse. Undergirding this sin is my tendency to view money as a way to retain control over my own life. I prop up money as an idol that will enable me to become wholly self-sufficient—needing to trust in no one but myself for my safety and security.

The prophet Jeremiah made it clear that idols are

"vanity . . . like scarecrows . . . worthless, a work of delu-
sion."[7] The deeper I fall into the idol worship of money
in the ways described above, the *less* I am fulfilled, not
more. The rich young ruler failed to recognize that he had
become blinded by his wealth. He mistakenly thought his
wealth provided him security, peace of mind, and status.
But God sees it differently.

Take a look at what the Bible says about wealth. Wealth
is fleeting: "it sprouts wings, flying like an eagle toward
heaven."[8] Even worse, our wealth causes us anxiety: "the
full stomach of the rich will not let him sleep."[9] Rather,
Scripture calls us to "delight yourself in the LORD, and
he will give you the desires of your heart."[10]

Our continual striving to control our finances causes
us *greater* anxiety, not less. The path to freedom is not
through more meticulous financial planning, but rather
through finding greater trust in God's promises as our
provider both now and in the future.

BUY ME A BOAT

The Beatles have a famous tune that reminds us that money
can't buy love.[11] But country music star Chris Janson wrote
a humorous song called "Buy Me a Boat," which points
out what money *can* buy. Specifically, money can buy a
boat, a truck, and an ice chest full of beer! He playfully
mocks the idea that money is pointless by highlighting
that life is pretty good when you can buy a few fun toys.[12]

Most of us have probably learned by now that the Beatles
and Chris Janson are both correct: money is not the ultimate

source of happiness, but it does help put food on the table and a roof over our family members' heads. Unfortunately, the expenses don't stop with food and shelter. Clothes, utilities, childcare, cell phones, TV, internet, travel, Christmas gifts, student loans, insurance, credit cards. The list goes on and on. And then there are unexpected expenses. I'm not sure there is a less-satisfying purchase than a new water heater when your old one suddenly goes out!

Making ends meet is tough. The Federal Reserve found that 46 percent of Americans would not be able to cover a $400 emergency expense, such as that new water heater, with cash savings, instead having to pay it off over time or borrow the money.[13] It appears our financial anxiety might be justified. For many families the numbers just don't add up.

Thankfully, we serve a God who, as Pastor Rick Warren said, "cares about our bills."[14] Providing for our families is rarely easy, but despite these challenges, God calls us to find peace in him rather than succumbing to our anxiety about money. Jesus said to "not be anxious about your life, what you will eat, nor about your body, what you will put on. For life is more than food, and the body more than clothing."[15]

Whenever I (Greg) think on this verse, I think of the pastor of the church I attended during grad school. He and his wife adopted eleven children and live on his middle-income salary in an expensive part of the country. Adopting eleven children was never their plan A, but it was God's plan. It's not always clear how they'll make ends meet, but somehow things always work out—often through incredible acts of generosity by members of the church. The pastor says, "Just like the apostle Paul, we've learned how to be satisfied with little and satisfied with much. We've learned to trust that God *will* provide, even if we don't always know exactly *how* he will do so."[16]

Rick Warren offers this challenge: "Do you trust God enough not to worry about your circumstances? Worry is really just a form of [idolatry], because every time you worry, you're saying, 'It all depends on me.' You must trust God with your life. As long as you love anything more than God, that thing or person or item will become a source of anxiety."[17]

To be clear, we cannot live however we want, spend all our money on frivolous things, end up broke, and then blithely say, "God will provide." God intends for us to *responsibly* utilize the resources he gives us for our provision. Further, the hard truth is that some people do not have all they need, often through no fault of their own. For instance, refugees fleeing a war-torn country, or a young child whose parents are addicted to drugs.

These are tough issues, often without clear answers. Poverty and suffering are part of our reality living in this broken and sinful world, and these challenges may never be fully remedied until Christ's return. In the meantime Christ's clear call is to trust in him regardless of our circumstances and to set our eyes upon what is to come, even as we acknowledge the legitimate struggles we and others face today.

SAVING LIKE A FOOL

Time magazine reported that worrying about finances is the number one cause of sleepless nights in America (as parents to three young children each, your humble coauthors beg to differ with this!).[18] While many of us worry about our monthly expenses, others worry more about the future. Namely, saving for retirement.

Responsibly saving for the future is certainly wise. But many of us take it too far, either by allowing future what-if scenarios to cause us immense anxiety or by oversaving in an attempt to control our own futures. Jesus told a parable about a man judiciously planning for his own retirement. His conclusion was startling:

> The land of a rich man produced plentifully, and he thought to himself, "What shall I do, for I have nowhere to store my crops?" And he said, "I will do this: I will tear down my barns and build larger ones, and there I will store all my grain and my goods. And I will say to my soul, 'Soul, you have ample goods laid up for many years; relax, eat, drink, be merry.'" But God said to him, "Fool! This night your soul is required of you, and the things you have prepared, whose will they be?" So is the one who lays up treasure for himself and is not rich toward God.[19]

Financial security had become the focus of the rich man's hopes and ambitions, displacing his relationship with God and stunting his ability to be generous. I (John) can relate. I've always loved saving. As a child I counted my coins and meticulously kept track of my finances on sticky notes. By age seventeen I was an experienced lawn mower and had saved up $10,000, one lawn at a time. By age twenty-five my wife and I were saving half our income each year and planned to retire by age forty. Because we consistently gave away 10 percent of our income, our relatives, friends, and even our church viewed us as financially mature Christians. But this was not necessarily true.

The parable of the rich fool turns the conventional American vision of wealth on its head. Even in the church, we tend to honor those who save responsibly and build wealth over time. Thus, God used this parable to break my heart.[20] I realized that despite my outward appearance of financial maturity, I was actually just as foolish as the rich man in the parable. My highest ambition in life was to accumulate wealth and retire early. I was blind to the greater joy, secure identity, and profound meaning that come from being "rich toward God" by wholeheartedly serving God and others with my financial resources.

Planning for the future is certainly wise.[21] But setting our hope and security in our savings is costly, depriving us of the joy of being generous here and now and dampening our trust in God, our one true provider.

PROMISE KEEPER

God delights in serving as our provider, meeting both our spiritual and material needs.[22] Let us not shy away from the reality, however, that millions of people worldwide face difficult financial struggles.

More than 700 million people live in extreme poverty worldwide; even in the United States, more than 40 million people live in poverty.[23] Nearly 900 million people suffer from hunger worldwide, of which more than 9 million will die from hunger this year alone—a number equivalent to the entire population of Michigan.[24] More than 780 million lack access to clean water, a problem that disproportionately impacts children.[25] This is on top of the millions of families who can be thankful for having enough food and water but lack the resources for adequate healthcare, quality education for their children, or safe living conditions.

Deuteronomy states that "there will never cease to be poor in the land."[26] This side of heaven, many of us will face regular struggles, financially and otherwise. So how should we think about God's promises to provide for our needs in light of the challenges many families face around the world?

First, we rejoice that we serve a God who *always* keeps his promises. Scripture tells us, "Not one word of all the good promises that the LORD has made to the house of Israel had failed; all came to pass," and "God is not a man, that he should lie. . . . Has he said, and will he not do it?"[27]

Second, we rest in the fact that God stands alongside us in our suffering. The prophet Isaiah wrote, "In all [Israel's] affliction he was afflicted, . . . in his love and in his pity he redeemed them" and "He gives strength to the weary and increases the power of the weak."[28] The apostle Paul wrote of the "God of all comfort, who comforts us in all our affliction."[29]

Third, we acknowledge that our spiritual needs supersede our material needs. Jesus spoke with a woman at a well: "Everyone who drinks of this water will be thirsty again, but whoever drinks of the water that I will give him will never be thirsty again. The water that I will give him will become in him a spring of water welling up to eternal life."[30]

Finally, we seek Christlikeness while we suffer, and while serving those who are suffering. James commands us to "count it all joy, my brothers, when you meet trials of various kinds, for you know that the testing of your faith produces steadfastness. And let steadfastness have its full effect, that you may be perfect and complete, lacking in nothing."[31]

Likewise, we must avoid judging or condemning those who are presently suffering, instead humbly serving them in their time of need. If we follow God's call to "share your bread with the hungry and bring the homeless poor into your house," and if we "see the naked" and "cover him," then "the glory of the LORD shall be your rear guard."[32] Indeed, when we serve others, God grants us the opportunity to *be* the evidence of his promise to supply his people's needs "according to his riches in glory"![33]

Corrie ten Boom, who assisted many Jewish families in escaping the Nazi Holocaust, wrote, "Never be afraid to trust an unknown future to a known God." Rather than succumbing to anxiety and despair in the midst of our suffering, we may lean on him, all the while acting as his hands and feet to supply provision to his people in need.

HAPPY-MAKING

Worrying about our money and hoarding our wealth is a waste of time at best and destructive to our relationship with God at worst. After all, no one has ever seen a U-Haul behind a hearse—that is, you can't take any of it with you![34] We must learn to trust God's plans for our money.

Early church father Basil of Caesarea (c. AD 330–379) wrote:

> And if you have only one remaining loaf of bread, and someone comes knocking at your door, bring forth the one loaf from your store, hold it heavenward, and say this prayer, which is not only generous on your part, but also calls for the Lord's pity: "Lord, you see this one loaf, and you know the threat of starvation is imminent, but I place your commandment before my own well-being, and from the little I have I give to this famished brother. Give, then, in return to me your servant, since I am also in danger of starvation. I know your goodness, and am emboldened by your power. You do not delay your grace indefinitely, but distribute your gifts when you will."[35]

Basil fully trusted in God's plans, even as he also understood that God's people *will* face challenging times in this life. His heart had been transformed by God's grace. Understanding God's grace grants us the freedom to be generous to others in trust of God's ultimate provision, and in gratitude for his generosity toward us.

Placing our trust in God enables us to push aside anxiety about our own needs and allows our hearts to be drawn toward God's calling to serve others. Sadly, many of us struggle to serve others financially: giving in America has declined steadily as a percentage of income for the last fifty years, despite the massive increase in quality of life enjoyed by most Americans over this period. These trends are true regardless of income bracket: families earning more than $150,000 per year give the same percentage of their income as do families earning less.[36] Christian Smith and Hilary Davidson, from authors of *The Paradox of Generosity*, determined that less than 3 percent of Americans give away 10 percent or more of their income, compelling them to state that "America has a generosity problem."[37]

American Protestants' Giving Rate by Year[38]

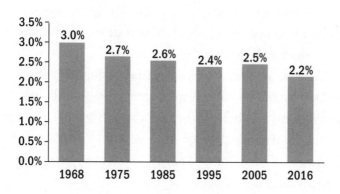

Many of us view giving money to the church as a religious duty or obligation. While God does command us to give, the word *duty* could not be a less accurate descriptor of God's vision for our generosity. When it comes to generosity, God wants something *for* us, not *from* us!

Jesus tells us, "It is more blessed to give than to receive" (Acts 20:35). Author Randy Alcorn stated that the Greek translation of the word *blessed* in this verse, *makarios*, is arguably more literally rendered as "happy-making."[39] The verse is more literally translated as "It is more *happy-making* to give than to receive." We receive incredible joy when we serve others with our financial resources. "Give, and it will be given to you. Good measure, pressed down, shaken together, running over, will be put into your lap. For with the measure you use it will be measured back to you."[40]

Moreover, our generosity toward others in this world translates to God's eternal generosity toward us in heaven. "Go, sell what you possess and give to the poor, and you will have treasure in heaven."[41] And "do not lay up for yourselves treasure on earth, . . . but lay up for yourselves treasures in heaven. . . . For where your treasure is, there your heart will be also."[42]

Indeed, Scripture directly relates caring for the poor to knowing God. "But if anyone has the world's goods and sees his brother in need, yet closes his heart against him, how does God's love abide in him?"[43] "He judged the cause of the poor and needy; . . . Is not this to know me? declares the LORD."[44]

God affirms that we should be generous not out of religious obligation, but rather because being generous offers us tremendous joy. "One gives freely, yet grows all the richer; . . . Whoever brings blessing will be enriched."[45] "Whoever sows bountifully will also reap bountifully. . . . God loves a cheerful giver."[46]

God doesn't need our money. He is sovereign and will ultimately accomplish his purposes. At the same time, God has elected to give each of us an important role to play here on earth. Therefore, generosity is better thought of as an opportunity given to us by God to step alongside him in the fulfillment of his kingdom. What plan for our money could be bigger or better than that?

ADRIANA AND PHIL: JOINING IN GOD'S STORY

Adriana and her husband, Phil, were working hard to build a life for themselves. Money was often tight, even a cause of stress. But Adriana and Phil were aligned on a clear vision of their future: to have children and to own a home in which to raise them.

"Saving for a house was a major goal of ours," Adriana elaborated. "There usually wasn't a lot of extra cash at the end of each month, so saving was difficult. But Phil and I knew we wanted to become homeowners." As is true with most families, Adriana and Phil occasionally faced difficult times financially. At one point they were forced to move into a small apartment attached to Adriana's mother's house. "There wasn't enough room for our son to play. We had some hard times for sure," Adriana said.

Although living in the small apartment was not ideal, Adriana and Phil were slowly but surely working their way toward a down payment for their own home. After three years of diligently saving they had accumulated $10,000. Adriana said, "We found a great little place, lined up a mortgage company, and the $10,000 we had saved was the perfect amount for the down payment. We were so excited!"

Meanwhile, God had different plans. Soon after lining up a mortgage for their new home, they met with a close friend from church who was going through a difficult divorce and was falling into debt. Adriana said, "I sensed God whisper to me, 'I gave you $10,000, and $5,000 is for your friend.' I was afraid to tell Phil about what I sensed God telling me, because I knew how hard he had worked to save up for our down payment. But I built up my courage and told Phil about my idea. Phil immediately responded that we should do it. We were so scared—but also excited! We just had to trust in God. If the house we were closing on was not for us, God would make that clear."

Adriana and Phil gave their friend the money. As a result, they could no longer fulfill their dream of buying a home. "The next week was very emotional—lots of tears and anxiety. We knew we did the right thing, but we were so stressed! One night I was sobbing in the bedroom of our little apartment, and in the middle of my tears, God stopped me. I felt his presence so strongly, and he said, 'Shhh . . . be still. I am with you.' I stopped crying. My husband asked me what was wrong. By the way, it is a sign of our emotional state at the time that Phil asked me what was wrong when I *stopped crying*! I said, 'God just told me to be still. I feel his peace.'"

The very next day, Adriana found an envelope in her mailbox from her mother. Inside was a check for $5,000! Adriana said, "I had been working with my mom for the past two years on a nonprofit venture she had started, all without pay. The same week God called us to give the $5,000 to our friend, God also spoke to my mom, saying, 'This money is for your daughter.' She gave us the money as thanks for my work with her nonprofit— without any knowledge that we had given money to our friend. Fortunately, there had been no other offers on the house, and we were now able to purchase our first home.

"So many people think we were irresponsible to give our friend the money. But I know that if we hadn't given it, our friend would have suffered, and we would have missed out on God's tremendous blessing. The way we now live is that we're going to help the people God asks us to help, never expecting anything in return. There might be temporary 'pain,' but we know God is our provider. He will be with us. And now we know the excitement of giving firsthand!"

Adriana and Phil's story reveals the tremendous adventure that awaits us when we cast away our financial anxiety and trust in God as our true provider. Money is one of several tools God uses to help us learn to trust him, and when we do trust him, he offers us the incredible joy of generosity in return. Not everyone who obeys God's call to generosity will receive an equivalent check in their mailbox the next week like Adriana and Phil did. But everyone who lives generously will experience God's love more deeply—for themselves and for others. As one of our mentors likes to say, we've never met a *former* generous giver!

TRUST AND JOY

The Bible includes more than twenty-three hundred verses about money, an indication that God knows how big a roadblock money can become in our walk with him.[47] Anxiety about what-if scenarios is perhaps the most common finance-related faith roadblock. This plays out in two ways:

- *What if I don't have enough right now?*
- *What if I don't have enough in the future?*

These fears stem from a lack of trust in God's promises to serve as our provider, meeting our physical needs now and, more importantly, meeting our spiritual needs into eternity.[48] As a result, we frequently hoard our resources and give sparingly in a vain attempt to fulfill our own needs.

Unfortunately, this strategy is doomed to backfire.[49] The writer of Ecclesiastes wrote, "He who loves money will not be satisfied with money."[50] Why do we allow ourselves to succumb to this temptation? Fear and anxiety compel us to adopt a mind-set of scarcity rather than a mind-set of abundance. We are deceived into embracing a false system for measuring our security, a system based on our net worth rather than in our Savior.

There is certainly nothing wrong with providing a nice life for our families. But for many of us, our bank accounts are getting in the way of our relationship with God. Our relationship with him must be our top priority.

Theologian Richard J. Foster wrote,

> If what we have we receive as a gift, and if what we have is to be cared for by God, and if what we have is available to others, then we will possess freedom from anxiety. This is the inward reality of simplicity. However, if what we have we believe we have gotten, and if what we have we believe we must hold onto, and if what we have is not available to others, then we will live in anxiety.[51]

Being generous in gratitude to Christ eliminates money's power over us. Generously sharing with others amplifies our trust in God and enables us to experience the unmatched joy of participating alongside Christ in serving his kingdom.[52]

Peter encouraged us to "cast all your anxiety on him because he cares for you."[53] Generosity is the method by which we cast our financial anxiety onto our provider. Generosity is also an act of discipleship. Theologian Walter Brueggemann wrote, "Discipleship is the renunciation of [money's] anxiety-producing power. Practically, that renunciation is performed as generosity that is free of greed and has no fear of scarcity."[54]

May we all cast away our fears and anxieties about money, learning to trust in God as our true provider. And in so doing, may we all experience the unique and lasting joy that God offers to those who live generously.

GETTING PRACTICAL: TRUSTING GOD WHILE I SAVE

Our fear and anxiety about money most directly intersect with our finances through how we save our money and how we handle debt. We save money now, because we desire to deploy those resources (plus interest) in the future. Interestingly, debt can be thought of the same way: we pay off debts now, because we desire to have fewer debt obligations (principal and interest) in the future. In other words, debt repayment helps someone get from negative net worth to zero, while saving helps someone get from zero net worth to positive. They are two sides of the same coin (pun intended). We often do both at the same time in life, such as saving for retirement while also paying off student loans.

How to wisely save money is a tricky area to evaluate from a spiritual perspective. On one hand, Scripture affirms that saving money and paying off debt is wise.[55] On the other hand, we are commanded not to be hoarders of wealth.[56] So how should we treat savings and debts?

A lack of savings may indicate either wisdom or foolishness, depending on the circumstances. If you save little because you spend every dollar you earn on consumer goods, the Bible calls you a "fool."[57] If you save little because you are boldly following God's clear call in your life, for example, as a missionary with a low salary, you are storing up treasure in heaven as you serve "the least of these."[58]

Likewise, a high rate of savings may indicate either wisdom or foolishness, depending on the circumstances. If you diligently save so that you may pay off your debts and prepare a down payment for an affordable home . . . that is wisdom.[59] If you diligently save because you love building wealth for yourself and are striving toward a leisurely early retirement . . . that is foolishness.[60]

Unfortunately, most people don't save much at all. In America the top 1 percent of earners save approximately 40 percent of their income, the top 10 percent of earners save approximately 10 percent of their income, and everybody else, statistically, saves nothing.[61] Whether you're in the top 1 percent or the bottom 10 percent, a clear savings plan can help you wisely manage the resources God has put in your hands.

There are three stages of saving, laid out in the diagram to the right. Biblical savings are goal-oriented savings, intended to meet our reasonable needs.

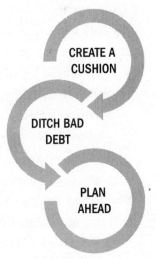

CREATE A CUSHION

DITCH BAD DEBT

PLAN AHEAD

Once those needs are met and as we achieve higher levels of wealth, our need to save diminishes, and we can focus more fully on kingdom generosity. If we fail to progress through these three stages, however, we handicap our ability to serve God with our finances.

Stage 1: Create a Cushion

If you have less than $2,000 in cash immediately available, whether in a checking or savings account, an envelope in your closet, or otherwise, then you are operating without a cushion. A flat tire, a roof leak, an unexpected health scare—any of these common events could put you into a crisis. In fact, a large study found that keeping $2,000 on hand is a key financial practice that contributes to an improved financial mind-set and sense of well-being.[62]

In Stage 1 we believe it is appropriate to aim to save steadily and even aggressively. Be sure to sustain your generosity toward God, however, even as you build this cushion. Not only is giving an act of obedience, but it also brings great joy that you don't want to miss.

Families who have been saving for some time may have emergency funds much larger than $2,000. Ideally, families would save three to six months' worth of expenses in a checking or savings account, enabling them to handle any emergency or engage in spontaneous acts of generosity with freedom and flexibility. Unfortunately, at least 40 percent of the American population has not completed Stage 1.[63] Saving $2,000 puts you in a much better position to absorb the type of unexpected major expense that occurs for all of us at some point in our lives.

So for our purposes, once you have $2,000 in cash or in a checking or savings account, you've graduated to Stage 2.

Stage 2: Ditch Bad Debt

Having debt means you have presumed upon the future to finance your present lifestyle. That can be a scary thought. If you're thirty years old and you have debt, you've said to your thirty-five-year-old self, "Hey, can I borrow some money? I'll pay you back—promise!"

All non-mortgage debts—car loans, student loans, unpaid credit card balances, and so forth—are "bad debts." They are not secured by an appreciating asset like a mortgage is and should be paid off as quickly as reasonably possible. They represent bondage in our lives and a potential stain upon our legacy.[64] Ideally, the only long-term debt we would have is an affordable mortgage loan, typically meaning that the balance is twice your income or less. For example, a family with a $100,000 income should seek a loan amount of $200,000 or less.[65]

A home should meet your family's needs without being excessive. We should choose a home for reasons of usefulness and need, rather than status or pride. We've found that even very mature Christians, even those who are extremely generous, admit to struggling with keeping their home purchase modest.

Also, please remember that online home-affordability

calculators assume that you are not a giver. Be wary of what they tell you. If you take out a loan for more than double your gross income, you'll likely be leveraged up to the point where you cannot invest generously in the kingdom of God, and you'll instead be loyal most of all to the "Kingdom of Your House."

> **Example:** If your income is $80,000 and you have $50,000 saved for a down payment, your home purchase budget is $50,000 + 2 x $80,000 = $210,000.

We should also note that wise planners seek to avoid taking on debt for an auto loan whenever possible. Once you pay off your cars, begin saving a monthly amount toward paying cash for your next car, even if the purchase is years away. (Note that these savings are in addition to your emergency fund—they are entirely separate and could be kept in their own savings account.) You might have to drive a clunker for a while, but it will pay off in the long run.

In Stage 2, aim to put as much as 20 to 40 percent of your income toward debt elimination. (20 percent may sound impossible. It's okay to start at a smaller number and work your way up.) Just as in Stage 1, never let your passion to eliminate debt squelch your desire to be generous. A major financial study of US households found that the number-one inhibitor of generosity was debt.[66] As you move toward freedom from debt, your generosity can increase.

Stage 3: Plan Ahead

If you're debt-free except for an affordable mortgage and have a cushion of $2,000 or more, then by God's grace you've achieved firm financial footing and can begin planning for the long-term future. Only about one-fourth of American households are in Stage 3.

When most people think long-term, they think ten, twenty, or thirty years into the future. That's wise. But God invites us to extend our horizon further. Where will your financial legacy be in one thousand years? One hundred thousand years? Eventually (after billions of years), even the sun will be burned out. But anything you've invested in God's kingdom is guaranteed to still be paying dividends.

In one experiment children were placed in a room with a marshmallow. They could eat the treat if they wanted. But if they waited long enough without eating it, they would be rewarded with two marshmallows. Children who can wait the longest demonstrate the most maturity, since they understand the idea of delayed gratification. Two marshmallows in five minutes is better than one marshmallow right now.

We have every ability to "eat our marshmallows" right now, here on earth. We can spend and save for ourselves, or build wealth to pass on to a future generation. That's a fine-tasting marshmallow. But God has put a better offer on the table: give generously—invest in God's kingdom—and he will give you rewards that last forever, into eternity. A gajillion marshmallows!

At Stage 3 you've achieved financial stability, and you now have a choice to make. Will you eat the marshmallows now? Or will you defer your gratification to heaven, where your reward for generosity will be immense?

To be clear, it is wise to continue saving some money in this stage. After all, you still need to pay off your home loan, and paying off your house early is a great idea. Plus, most households have wise goals that require further savings such as a secure retirement in old age or college education for children.

The prominence and focus of savings, however, should begin to diminish as wealth increases. You may start Stage 3 putting as much as 40 percent of your income toward savings and paying off your mortgage. That savings rate should decline over the years as you approach the idea of "enough." In this stage it is vitally important to be cautious not to allow your passion for saving to eclipse your passion for giving. Remember that Jesus told the parable of the rich fool to warn against this very issue. At some point, your savings rate may drop to 0 percent, but your giving rate can continue to climb as you take on bigger and bigger projects for God's kingdom.

Our families are in the beginning of Stage 3, and we each still save 25–35 percent of our incomes. We also give away 15–25 percent of our gross incomes. But we look to mentors who are further into Stage 3, who have stopped saving and now give away half or even more of their incomes. We hope to do the same someday.

The focus of Stage 3 is eternity. Your life on earth

will be gone before you know it. God has given you three eternal goals: serving the poor, strengthening believers, and saving the lost. (We'll learn more about these goals in chapter 5.) Pursue these goals with all your might, for the glory of God!

> Many people track their net worth, but have you considered tracking your cumulative lifetime giving? Watching the number grow can be motivating. Could you give away $100,000 over the course of your lifetime? $1 million?

Summary of the Three Stages of Saving

STAGE 1
CREATE A CUSHION

Save $2,000 in cash, checking, or savings accounts

STAGE 2
DITCH BAD DEBT

Pay off all debts except for an affordable mortgage.

Mortgage should be less than 2 times your gross household income.

STAGE 3
PLAN AHEAD

Begin giving more aggressively than ever before.

Consider paying off your home early.

Consider longer-term goals such as retirement, college funding, etc.

APPLICATION

We recommend "Trust In You" by Jeremy Camp as a great song to accompany this chapter's application exercise.

Download or recreate the tables below in your journal. Consider a one-year period. It could be this calendar year or the last twelve months, whichever is easier for you to think about. Fill in the amount of money you've saved and paid toward debts on an annual basis.

My Savings: How much did I save over the last year?

Category	Note	Annual Amount Saved
Cash Accounts	Did you save up any cash this year?	
Retirement Funds	How much did you save toward retirement this year? Include company contributions or matches in this number.	
College Funds	Did you save toward future educational costs?	
Car Fund	Did you save toward future car purchases?	
Investments	Did you save by buying stocks, bonds, or other investments?	
Total Annual Savings	Add up the rows above to get your total annual savings amount.	

My Debts: How much money did I spend servicing debts over the last year?

Category	Note	Annual Debt Repaid
Principal and Interest on Mortgage	Take your monthly mortgage payment of principal and interest, and multiply by twelve.	
Student Loan	Take your monthly student loan payment of principal and interest, and multiply by twelve.	
Other Debt	Amount paid on things like your car loan, student loan, credit card debt, etc.	
Other Debt		
Other Debt		
Total Annual Debt Payments	Add up the rows above to get your total annual debt payments.	

In personal finance we learn that Net Worth = Assets − Debts. We can increase our net worth both by saving money (increasing assets) and repaying debts (reducing debts). We will now add together our Total Annual Savings and Total Annual Debt Payments from the tables above in order to calculate how much of our income we are allocating toward savings and debts each year.

Once you divide your Total Annual Savings and Debt Payments by your Total Family Income, you've calculated your Savings and Debt Payment Rate. Think of this as your "Wealth Building Ratio"—the higher this fraction, the more you are allocating your income toward building financial security for the future.

Total Savings Rate Calculation:
Annual Savings + Annual Debt Payment

	Category	Note	Amount
	Total Annual Savings	From My Savings table above	
+	Total Annual Debt Payments	From My Debts table above	
=	Total Annual Savings and Debt Payments		
÷	Total Family Income	From page 29	
=	Annual Savings and Debt Payment Rate	% of Family Income used for savings or debt repayment	

Early in life, it may be appropriate to have a high rate of savings and debt payments. In Stage 1 and Stage 2, we believe 20–40 percent is a reasonable range to aim for. As you enter Stage 3 your need for further savings and debt elimination may diminish over the years, allowing you to save less and less and give more and more.

Write in your journal the stage you are in and your Savings and Debt Payment Rate:

Stage 1 | Stage 2 | Stage 3
My Savings and Debt Payment
Rate:_____ percent

Plot yourself on the Savings and Debt Payment Rate graph below and see where you fall, relative to our recommended ranges. What do you notice? The graph is a suggested norm, not a rule that must be followed.[67]

Reflect on the following scripture as you consider what changes God might have in store for your savings plan:

"Do not lay up for yourselves treasures on earth, where moth and rust destroy and thieves break in and steal, but lay up for yourselves treasures in heaven, where neither moth nor rust destroys and where thieves do not break in and steal. For where your treasure is, there your heart will be also" (Matt. 6:19–21).

Savings and Debt Repayment Rate

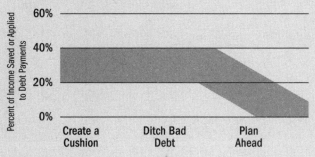

5

FROM INDIFFERENCE TO LOVE

Love is the overflow of joy in God that meets the needs of others.

—*John Piper*

We move from **Pride** to **Gratitude**
We move from **Coveting** to **Contentment**
We move from **Anxiety** to **Trust**
We move from Indifference to Love

TRUE CONFESSION? I (John) am not a very compassionate person. I once asked a college friend if I should pray for God to help me care more about other people, or if I should just accept that I don't. My focus on myself was keeping me from having concern for the well-being of others. This kind of deeply rooted indifference made giving tricky. We often assume we should give to things that we care about deeply. But what if we just don't care at all?

I eventually realized that I had the process backward. We shouldn't give to things because we care about them deeply. Rather, we should give to things because *God* cares about them deeply. Giving often starts as an obedient step of faith before it blossoms into joyful love over time.

Jesus said, "Where your treasure is, there your heart will be also."[1] He meant that wherever we send our money, our feelings and emotions will eventually go there too. If we send money toward the things God cares about, our hearts will start to look more like God's. Generosity is just a means to an end; it is an investment in the love of God for us and for others.

For example, I never really cared about modern-day slavery until I began giving to International Justice Mission. Slowly, over time, I began to yearn for freedom for everyone in captivity. I never cared much about children trapped in poverty until I began giving to Compassion International. Slowly, over time, I began to ache for every child in need to be fed, educated, and taught about Jesus. And I never cared much about people who didn't have the Bible until I sponsored a Bible translation project through the Seed Company. Now I have a deeper passion that all people on earth would be able to read Scripture in their native language.

My heart was often cold and indifferent to others. But giving is like a seed planted in the barren soil of indifference. If we plant in faith, love will begin to grow and will displace our indifference. How do we obtain the true riches of love? We give in faith, asking God to reshape our hearts in the process.

If a marriage counselor is helping a couple in a bad marriage, he or she would never tell the struggling couple to wait until they feel more love before serving each other. The counselor would say, "Start acting as if you're in love, and the feelings will follow." Giving is the same way. If we want God's heart, we give to the things he cares about. He honors our steps of faith by changing our hearts and aligning our passions with his.

This is a process. It took me four years of consistent giving to the poor before God awakened a heart for the poor in me. But our faithfulness and obedience, in joy, does lead to heart change. In this chapter, we'll see this process of heart change play out for a woman named Sheila.

SHEILA'S SAVINGS

Daydreaming in her Chicago office, Sheila could hear her dad's voice as if it were in the room with her: "No. We can't afford it. We must protect what our family has."

She remembered hearing those words a thousand times during her childhood in China. Her parents had survived the Cultural Revolution, meaning that life was marked by scarcity, frugality, and financial conservatism. Family was first, and savings were the key to the future.

Pulling her mind back to the present, Sheila refocused on her dual twenty-inch computer monitors displaying company financials in Microsoft Excel. The financial model she was building was difficult and complex, and she needed to have it done before leaving work. But it had been an exhausting day, and her mind soon began to wander again. This time she remembered the first time she learned about sweatshops. At seven years old, a friend had told her about these factories, where workers—her neighbors or friends—might be expected to work tireless, endless hours for miniscule wages. She had even prayed a childlike prayer: "God, someday I'd like to help people trapped in places like that."

After the Cultural Revolution, her parents had immigrated to the United States. Sheila had finished high school in California before heading off to a great college, where she graduated with honors. She'd landed this job in finance and was now making it in America on her own, even earning a couple of promotions within her first few years on the job. True to her upbringing, she had been saving as much as she could along the way.

In fact, Sheila's annual bonus would be coming soon. It had been a good year for her and for the company. Her peers were already discussing international vacations, new cars, and other splurges. Of course, Sheila would sock every dollar away. *Life is good*, she thought to herself, imagining the potential size of her own bonus. She had a huge nest egg built up for a twenty-nine-year-old, and she loved to play out in her mind the different ways it could equip her for the future.

Someday she hoped to be married, put money down on a house, and—in the distant future—retire comfortably. With almost $200,000 in the bank at this early age, she was ready for whatever life might throw her way.

We'll soon return to Sheila's journey. But first, let's take a quick detour and examine some challenging facts about generosity in our world today.

LOVING LESS THAN WE THINK

We tend to think highly of ourselves. In fact, 93 percent of Americans rate themselves as above-average drivers.[2] Due to a cognitive bias known as illusory superiority, we think of ourselves as better than others, even when we aren't. This is true not only for driving skills but also for generosity. *Everyone* considers themselves to be "a generous person." But are we?

The following chart shows responses from millennial Christians to a large survey.[3] Seventy percent claim to be generous with money, but only 16 percent gave at least fifty dollars to a church or charity in the prior year. It's hard to imagine how someone can be classified as "generous" if they gave away less than fifty dollars in a whole year. (By the way, don't blame it all on us millennials; stats for other generations were similar.)

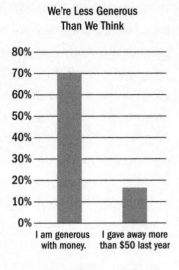

We're Less Generous Than We Think

Jesus told a story intended to shake us out of this cognitive bias and move us to action in our giving (Luke 16:19–31). He explained that a rich man had splendid clothes and fine food in his beautiful home. Outside was a homeless beggar, Lazarus, covered in festering sores, hungry, and neglected. The rich man never actively harmed Lazarus, but he never tried to help him either. Both eventually died. Lazarus went to heaven; the rich man found himself in eternal torment. He asked for relief and was reminded that he had his share of comfort during his life on earth. He asked for his living brothers to be warned, but he was told that if they hadn't listened to the Scriptures' command to love the needy, they wouldn't listen to a message from the afterlife. The basic message to the rich man was: "You knew what to do, and you missed your chance!"

Notice that Jesus didn't ask whether the rich man felt "called" to help the poor. We can almost hear the rich man telling a friend, "You know, I never felt *led* to serve the poor. I know that some people really care about poverty, but it's just never been my thing." He almost surely thought of himself as a generous man, and his dinner parties were probably fantastic (it's easy to be generous to our close friends). Despite this, he still failed to hear God's instruction to serve the poor.

The sobering question that Jesus wants us to ask after hearing this story is, "Am I the rich man?"

As a thought experiment, let's imagine that the entire world population has been reduced to just ten families who live on a single street together, in ten successive homes from poorest to richest.[4]

On one end of the street, a family with no home at all is enslaved or facing starvation. The second family, their neighbor, lives in a leaky lean-to with a dirt floor, eats a basic porridge every day, and hangs on to survival, walking barefoot down to the creek to get dirty water that they drink and bathe in. Those two families are "Lazarus."

The middle six houses, representing most families in the world today, have basic cement homes of improving quality as we progress down the street. Their roofs usually don't leak, although a cold draft creeps through the walls in winter and most of them can't afford air conditioning, so the summer can be sweltering. These homes have running water, bicycles or mopeds for transportation, and their electricity works most of the time. These families own conveniences like toothbrushes, refrigerators, and shoes. Their lives are fairly stable and healthy, although they work incredibly hard and cannot yet imagine owning a car or taking a leisurely vacation.

Finally, down on the wealthy end of the street there are two families that amaze their neighbors by earning tens of thousands of dollars per year. Their homes have multiple bedrooms, advanced heating and cooling, and full kitchens. Whereas the poorest family walks barefoot to fetch water, the richest household has a swimming pool full of clean water for purely recreational purposes! These wealthy families have garages with cars parked in them, communicate by smartphone, and leave for a basic vacation once or twice per year. They may not have millions of dollars, but they never miss a meal due to hunger or have to walk to work or school barefoot.

This table shows a statistically accurate picture of what each household would earn (adjusted for cost-of-living differences across geographies).[5]

1	2	3	4	5	6	7	8	9	10
$1k	$2k	$2.5k	$3k	$4k	$6k	$8k	$12k	$30k	$54k

For every dollar household #1 spends, household #10 has over fifty dollars to work with! Which house is most representative of the one you would be living in, if this were your street? Go ahead and circle the house that is closest to yours. If you're reading this book, we're going to guess that it's the richest or second-richest. Perhaps your family earns much more than $54,000 per year, meaning that your earnings are beyond what even the richest family's would be! If your family makes at or above the median income in the United States, you may be surprised to learn that, among ten randomly selected families from around the world, you'd likely be the richest. Even those who might feel poor in America—those earning $30,000 per year—are among the world's most financially blessed people.

The point here is not to feel guilt if you're financially blessed. Indeed, Paul writes that God "richly provides us with everything to enjoy."[6] The Cortines family, like the richest family on our fictitious street, owns a swimming pool and we receive it as God's gracious gift. However, we are deeply aware of what a luxurious gift it is, and we seek to cultivate empathy, compassion, and love toward the families on the other end of the street—and that love must manifest itself in tangible acts of generosity.

Jesus spoke in strong language about the rich man whose family would have also been on the wealthy end of the street. He claimed that those who are blessed with great provision—meaning those whose families earn perhaps $30,000 per year or more in the modern economy—have a special requirement to generously share with people facing starvation and lack. It's not about fairness, or socialism, or utilitarian ethics, or honor. It's about love—a love that seeks to love others as we love ourselves, just as Jesus taught us.

Remember, our feelings are not the important factor. Our actions are what counts. The vast majority of readers, and these authors, are the rich man. God invites us to love Lazarus. We don't necessarily have to feel compassion all the time (I still struggle with this myself). We just have to live and give on behalf of others. When our passion for giving to the needy is smaller than God's love for the needy, we face a faith-gap. All it takes to fill in the gap is a step of bold faith in generosity—the kind of step that Sheila would be taking before she knew it.

SHEILA'S UNEXPECTED VACATION

Sheila wondered whether she had made a mistake as her plane came in for a bumpy landing in Port-au-Prince. She thought back a few weeks, remembering how she got here.

"Well, are you going to come?" Amy was standing at Sheila's office door, wearing a broad smile. "It's going to be amazing!"

Amy had been applying friendly pressure to have Sheila join an upcoming trip to Haiti to visit various ministries and gain exposure to what true poverty looks like. Finally, this time she caved. "Okay . . . sure, Amy. Send me details. I think I'll join you."

Now here she was, unsure what to expect during her visit to the most impoverished country in the Western Hemisphere. She had no idea that the next few days would change her life forever.

Sheila was captivated by the people. They weren't statistics, opportunities, or names on a page. They were human beings with faces, hands, hopes, dreams, and dignity. Unfortunately, the sad desperation of inescapable poverty hung over them all. As the trip concluded, Shelia thought, *I'll never be able to unsee this.*

When she got home, she immediately began giving to one of the ministries she'd visited that provided employment to local women, enabling them to sell handcrafted products to American retailers. Her love of saving was now pitted against her newfound love for the women she had encountered in Haiti, but her excitement for giving continued to build.

A few days later, she told her parents all about her experience over the phone. The line was silent. After a few long moments, her mother flatly offered, "Well, we hope you've gotten that out of your system."

Sheila's parents were Christians, but their focus on family provision precluded any inkling of generosity toward outsiders. Like the rich man, their notion of generosity was constrained to a tight social or family circle and did not include the poor. Sheila was grateful for their hard work and immigration to America, but saddened by their scornful reaction to her generosity. She knew that saving was important, but God was stirring something deeper in her as she began to give.

Even if our family or culture tells us not to give to the spiritually and physically needy, God consistently beckons us to give it a try.

THE INVITATION

"Hey, Daddy. What'cha doin'? Can I help?" My (John's) four-year-old has asked me this question a thousand times. No matter what my answer is, he wants in. Fixing a curtain rod, restringing the Weed Eater, sending an email, cooking breakfast, running to the store. He wants in on all of it!

Does he love curtain rods, emails, or shopping trips? Not really. He loves *me*. He wants to be with me, to be taught by me, and to receive the loving affirmation that only a father can give, as we take on a project together. And you know what? I love when he comes to me like this. Even though I'm an imperfect dad, I nearly always invite him in.

Our Father God is the perfect dad, and like a good earthly dad, he loves when we approach him. He invites us into what he's doing. What if we approached God with the enthusiasm of a four-year-old?

"Hey, God, what'cha doin'? Can I help?"

God has lovingly already said yes. He's adopted us as his children through Jesus and has invited us into his work. He answers us, "Yes, my child. Here's my to-do list today. Do you want to help? I was hoping you'd join me."

GOD'S TO-DO LIST

Throughout Scripture, God reveals three top priorities— three big things he is up to in the world. He invites us to help with each of these, and we get to join our eternal dad in doing his work. As we take on these tasks, God grows our capacity to love, breaking us free from indifference.[7]

Task 1: Serve the Poor (Mercy and Justice)

Christians throughout the centuries have been moved by God's heart for the poor. Remember early church father

Basil of Caesarea? He preached a sermon on this more than sixteen hundred years ago:

> I must not be rich while they go begging, nor enjoy good health without attempting to heal their wounds, nor have abundant food, good clothing, and a roof under which I can rest, unless I offer them a piece of bread and give them, as I can, part of my clothing and shelter under my roof.

These were more than empty words. Basil grew up wealthy but sold off the majority of his inheritance to serve the poor in his region. Many other Christians have done similar things through the ages. Why do Christians care so much about the poor? Because God does.

Psalm 113, for example, describes the glory and grandeur of God in his heavenly majesty, but then takes a turn, claiming that he "looks far down" to the earth and "raises the poor from the dust and lifts the needy from the ash heap." Psalm 68 identifies God as the "Father of the fatherless and protector of widows." Psalm 82 goes further. In a poetic contest of the gods, our God is the greatest god not because of his omnipotent power, but rather because he gives "justice to the weak and the fatherless" and "rescue[s] the weak and the needy."

Jesus instructed his disciples to love their neighbors as they loved themselves. We don't often stop and think about the implications of this, but the concept came alive for us (John and Megan) when we learned that our sponsored child in Honduras had an eye problem. We felt a personal connection to this little four-year-old girl and knew that she lacked the resources for proper medical care. Would we spend $1,000 on our own child's eye? Yes, without hesitation. And, for the first time ever, we felt God's love well up so strong within us for *someone else's child*. We quickly wrote to the ministry, asking for their help in determining whether our financial assistance could solve this medical problem. We would pay any cost to help her.

Jesus affirmed the importance of serving the poor, even telling a parable about how the cups of cold water we give to, or withhold from, the poor are being counted by God.[8] In his story, those who fail to serve the poor are thrown into hell! The Bible teaches salvation by grace alone, through faith alone. We can't earn our way to heaven by doing good things. So why did Jesus tell this story?

Perhaps Jesus is telling us that we never truly know him as Savior and Lord unless we know him well enough to figure out that his business is in caring for the downtrodden. As Jesus' brother James wrote, pure religion is found in caring for orphans and widows in their time of need.[9]

Claiming to be a Christian but not giving to the poor is like claiming to be a chef but not knowing how to cook. It just doesn't make sense; it's a contradiction of terms. Christians care for the needy; it's in our spiritual DNA. As the church father John Chrysostom (c. AD 347–407) put it, "Do not tell me you cannot look after others. If you are Christians, what is impossible is for you to not watch after them."[10]

Task 2: Save the Lost (Evangelism)

More than once, Jesus' instruction after helping or healing someone was, "Go and sin no more." What a strange thing to say! Why not, "Enjoy your life! Be blessed!" One time before he healed a paralyzed man, he said, "Son, your sins are forgiven." Why would he say this?

Jesus cared for the whole person. He fed the hungry and healed the sick, but he did so in the context of holistic healing, including an invitation to enter the kingdom of God. He knew that there was limited value in making people more comfortable in life if they were still hurtling toward eternal separation from God. He wanted to truly save them, forever. When he looked at a paralyzed person, his first thought was, *They need forgiveness for their sins*. Physical pain and suffering is secondary to our spiritual reality.

In fact, Jesus' final instruction to his disciples, known as the Great Commission, was this:

> Go therefore and make disciples of all nations, baptizing them in the name of the Father and of the Son and of the Holy Spirit, teaching them to observe all that I have commanded you.[11]

Jesus had a clear vision that his gospel would reach the ends of the earth, giving all people a chance to respond to God's invitation. Today, two thousand years after Jesus walked the earth, we are within reach of this goal. You may not be called specifically to go to the edges of the world to share the gospel, but you can give generously to support those who do.

Bible translation provides one unique perspective into global evangelism. The Bible has been successfully translated into thousands of languages, but there are still approximately nineteen hundred spoken languages on earth that have no Bible at all.[12] Thousands of people are working diligently to continue translation, and hundreds of thousands of generous believers are funding this work. Many believe that the last Bible translator has been born—that we will finish the task in our lifetime.[13]

Millions of people still wait for someone to bring them liberation from their greatest poverty of all: separation from God. They need the Bible. They need churches and pastoral care. They need a fellowship of believers.

In our postmodern culture, it's not popular to assert claims of truth or to imagine that someone needs to have their belief system changed. Yet, two plus two still equals four, and Jesus is still the only way to God. To deny this is to deny the heart of Christianity, and if we really believe in Jesus, we must believe that his message of hope is a message for all mankind. Reconciliation with God, through Jesus, is the most important thing anyone can ever experience.

Despite the clarity and force of the Great Commission, less than 0.1 percent of Christian income is given to global foreign missions (less than eight dollars per person, per year).[14] The truest love we can show our neighbors around the globe is to bring them an opportunity to know the God who made them and loves them.

Task 3: Strengthen Believers (Discipleship)

The first half of the Great Commission is baptism, or salvation. The second half is "teaching them to observe all that I have commanded you." This is the primary and ongoing task of our local churches. Jesus cares deeply about his followers having a maturing, growing, healthy faith that guides their daily lives. In fact, Jesus clearly instructs that those who provide spiritual instruction are to be paid well: "Let the elders who rule well be considered worthy of double honor, especially those who labor in preaching and teaching. For the Scripture says, 'You shall not muzzle an ox when it treads out the grain,' and, 'The laborer deserves his wages.'"[15]

Consider writing down your favorite giving experience each year. Over time you will be able to look back and see how God has blessed you and others through your generosity! You may even share these stories with your children or other close friends as a testimony to God's goodness.

Many church staff have taken on their jobs as a response to God's calling on their lives, forgoing significantly higher earning power to serve God's people. In a large church, the senior pastor and executive pastor are the CEO and COO of a multimillion-dollar organization. They hire and fire staff, set strategy, establish a vision, carry culture, manage board relationships, and fight fires every week. Did I mention that they need to have an excellent sermon ready every weekend? And they do all this while potentially earning half what they could be earning in the private sector!

The church is God's plan for the world—his chosen vehicle to grow his family, and to serve the poor and save the lost. Without our local churches, we would have no place to take our children for regular worship, no steady stream of biblical teaching to sit under, no gathering place for fellow believers. God is all-in for the church. Are you?

We should ask the same questions of our churches that we'd ask of any nonprofit regarding how diligently they use their resources. But we should also know that we have a huge head start as potential supporters of our churches, relative to other nonprofits. We're already conducting due diligence—we visit every week, we know the staff, and we witness much of the work firsthand. Most of us know far less about the charities we support than we know about our local churches.

Here are two basic questions to ask as you consider generous support for your local congregation:

- **Is my church on-mission?** Does my church strengthen believers, building them up to maturity in Christ? Also, does my church have initiatives to look outward and serve the poor and save the lost? (Many churches we admire give 10–15 percent or more of their budget outwardly, to mission work or to serve the poor globally.)

- **Is my church leadership accountable to others, financially and personally?** Is there a board of elders who oversee the leadership? To whom are the pastoral leaders accountable? Some large churches are members of the Evangelical Council for Financial Accountability (ECFA). Other churches publish their budgets for members to see. Whatever the methods, a church should ensure that its leadership and budget are subject to outside scrutiny. (Note: this may not mean that *you* have a right to see the budget. It just means that there should be a board, an auditing agency, or some equivalent mechanism to ensure accountability.)

If your church is on-mission for God and has accountable leadership, you can give with confidence. If it's not, you might prayerfully consider either advocating for change or finding a new church home.

What About "Other" Giving?

We've discussed the three clear giving tasks in Scripture, but there are also times we've had to face the dilemma of whether we should give to other causes. We've each been modest supporters of our alma maters, we both enjoy the arts and museums, and we're not opposed to medical research or many other great causes.

As we've each prayed through this issue, we've been convicted that as Christians our primary focus in giving has to be on the tasks God has clearly given us, in his

113

infinite wisdom and goodness. So while we might send fifty dollars to our alma mater as a token of appreciation, we'll save the vast majority of our giving for the big three tasks: serving the poor, saving the lost, and strengthening believers.

In fact, St. Augustine—a giant of the early Christian faith and one of the most respected theologians of all time—addressed this very issue seventeen hundred years ago. Wealthy Roman citizens were joining the church, and "love of the city" was pitted against "love of the poor." These experienced philanthropists were used to giving to art projects, civic activities, and public buildings, but Augustine challenged them to instead take up the Christian mission to serve the poor in Jesus' name.

GIVING: A LOOOOONG-TERM INVESTMENT

Knowing that God wants us to lovingly give might be enough of a reason to comply. However, he's wired us to care about incentives and rewards. Thankfully, generosity pays off, big time.

Many people labor their whole lives for things that are gone forever, after one brief, effervescent sparkle. Our house, our emergency fund, our lifestyle, our 401k—we may think of these treasures as secure. By contrast, we imagine that when we give money away, it's gone. But from the perspective of eternity, the opposite is true.

All we have here and now is a puff of smoke, gone before we can even fully embrace it, slipping continuously from our fingers like sand on the seashore. Have you ever had a birthday and thought, *How has a whole year gone by already?* Our lives will be over soon. Moses wanted us to remember this, praying, "Teach us to number our days that we may get a heart of wisdom."[16] Wise people know that their time on earth will soon be past. But the New Testament teaches us to savor our unique opportunity to invest in eternal treasure. Paul writes that those who have resources should give generously, so they can be "storing up treasure for themselves as a good foundation for the future."[17]

Salvation is equal for all followers of Christ, but rewards are not. Some of us will be wealthier in heaven, and the basis for this inequality is what we do here on earth. We don't know exactly what that will look like, but we have some indications from Scripture. Jesus said that "many who are first will be last, and the last first."[18] Indeed, Paul wrote that when we enter heaven, "the inspection will be thorough and rigorous. You won't get by with a thing. If your work passes inspection, fine; if it doesn't, your part of the building will be torn out and started over. But you won't be torn out; you'll survive— but just barely."[19] Paul asserted, along with Jesus, that our *access* to heaven is a free gift of grace, but our *reward* in heaven is determined by our actions here on earth.

This is a limited-time offer. When you die, your opportunity to invest is gone.[20] But today the door is wide open. You can trade temporary, earthly dollars for eternal, heavenly rewards that will never, ever, ever, go away. It's a no-brainer!

Piling on with our theme, Proverbs 19 asserts that "he who is generous to the poor lends to the LORD" (v. 17). In other words, when we give to the poor, the God of all creation says, "Hey, I owe you one!" We may not fully understand the mechanism of heavenly rewards, but we have the promise of God. He's worth trusting as we make investments in eternity.

As we turn back to Sheila's story, we'll see that she would soon have the opportunity to make just such an investment.

SHEILA'S ETERNAL INVESTMENT

Sheila and Amy couldn't believe it. The ministry they loved and supported was going to be shut down.

Apparently the ministry had missed a deadline for a shipment due to a major American retailer. Contractually, this meant the retailer could fine them $250,000! They had pled their case to the retailer, explained that they were a ministry serving impoverished women, and tried every other avenue they could think of. It seemed that nothing was going to work.

The $250,000 fine was simply beyond what the ministry could afford to pay. It seemed unreal, but their only option might be to shut their doors, consigning all the women they served to return to unemployment.

With this news ringing fresh in her mind, Sheila set off for a conference called the Celebration of Generosity. This was a gathering of five hundred radical, all-in Christian givers hosted by Generous Giving (the organization

John works for) and designed to encourage givers and share stories of the joy of generosity. As she prayerfully engaged with the Lord that weekend, he began to stir up a crazy idea.

I have just over $200,000 sitting in a savings account now, Sheila thought. *That's almost the full amount they need*. It was her life savings, squirrelled away diligently, dollar by dollar, as she had lived frugally and stashed every bonus. It would be unthinkable to part with it. What would her parents say? What if she needed the money?

She would push the thought away, but it kept coming back. Somehow, her love for the women in Haiti and her desire to follow God's prompting began to outweigh her fear and her desire for self-preservation. Finally, she made up her mind.

Shelia emptied her checking and savings accounts the next week, taking her funds down to zero. She said that at the moment she delivered the check, she felt "peace and freedom, rather than fear or regret."

As she reflected on this event, she realized that the ministry she had given her savings to keeps people out of sweatshops. God spoke quietly to her heart. "You may have forgotten your prayer at age seven," he whispered, "but I did not. You've helped these women and rescued them from desperate conditions. I answered your childhood prayer by giving you a part in this story!"

The cost of the gift has been high. It was everything she had. In fact, Sheila has not told her parents. She knows they would react in an extremely negative way.

Although that aspect of it has been painful, she rejoices in partnering with God to shine a light on those living in darkness, in Jesus' name!

Bible scholar Sondra Wheeler has reflected extensively on the soaring joys and the intense earthly heartaches that discipleship with Jesus in our finances can bring. Her comments are an apt summary of the adventure that Sheila and many other believers have lived out:

> The way to life is first a way to death; it is a journey on which there can be no provision for baggage. The costs are appalling, paid in severed human relationships as well as in silver, and the capacity to bear them is the work of God and not of human beings. While the present rewards of the journey are real and rich, they are also vulnerable; only under the eschatological horizon is this way revealed unambiguously as the road to life.[21]

We find inspiration in the radical obedience and sacrifice Sheila made, driven by the love in her heart. She overcame her own fears and self-interest to choose the road to life, and we know God is thrilled to lead her on this adventure of grace.

WHERE DO I START?

So, every Christian has three interlocking tasks in front of them: serving the poor, saving the lost, and strengthening believers. Investing in these tasks is an investment in the true riches of heaven.

Having spoken to countless people about giving, the most common objection at this point is usually, "Okay, I want to jump in! But I don't really know any poor people. And most of my friends are Christian." Well, here's the good news. You don't need to start your own ministry from scratch; you just need to find a good organization to support. Your gift to a highly effective nonprofit can have a huge impact, and all it requires is a few clicks online or dropping a check in the mail.

Remember, the goal is to walk in relationship with God, and to ask him, "Hey, Daddy . . . what'cha doin'?" He will invite us into his mission!

APPLICATION

We recommend "Do Something" by Matthew West as a great song to accompany this chapter's application exercise.

Love is the capstone of God's true riches for our financial lives, and gospel-centered generosity is a tool he uses to move us toward love. Generosity is the outward fruit and the visible evidence of love. We each walk along a continuum of generosity, from coldhearted stinginess on one extreme, to the self-giving, joyful love of Jesus on the other. If we're walking with Jesus, we'll be growing along this continuum for our entire lives.

To start our reflections on giving, please step back to recount all the giving you've done, either in the past twelve months or in a full calendar year, whichever is easiest to think about. Remembering all the giving you have done will prime your thinking for the quiz that follows.

My Household Giving

Download or recreate in your journal the tables below. List all your annual giving. Sum it up, and divide by your income from page 29 to find your giving rate.

Gift to:	Note	Annual Giving
Example: My Church	Monthly giving, $300/mo	$3,600
Total	Sum of all rows	

Giving Rate Calculation

Total Giving (from above)		Total Family Income (from page 29)		Giving Rate
Ex: $3,600	÷	$ 40,000	=	9 %
$	÷	$	=	%

Consider the giving you listed in the "Giving Rate Calculation" table. Does your giving contribute toward each of the three tasks that Jesus invites us to work on? Read the following questions, and write some thoughts below or in your journal:

1. How does my giving serve the poor by bringing mercy and justice?

_____

_____

_____

_____

2. How does my giving strengthen believers, helping them grow into maturity as disciples?

_____

_____

_____

_____

3. How does my giving save the lost by proclaiming the gospel to those who don't know Jesus as Lord and Savior?

_____

_____

_____

_____

4. Which task do I invest the most in? Which task do I invest the least in?

_____

_____

_____

_____

_____

As we take steps of faith in our giving journey, God shapes our hearts. The following quiz will help you self-diagnose where you are in your own giving journey—an emerging giver, a committed giver, or an extravagant giver. Most American Christians are what we refer to as emerging givers, and we estimate that just 5 percent or less are extravagant givers.

As you take the quiz, it may be obvious what the most "holy" answer is, but please answer honestly. We'll tell you up front that C is the best answer, but we probably all have some A answers! Without honesty the exercise is pointless. We readily admit that we are not proud of our own answers to a few of these questions. That's okay, and we trust God to shape us to look more like him as we grow in our love, through generosity.

1. The main reason I give money away is:
   a. I feel a sense of duty or obligation.
   b. I have a growing desire to have an impact for good.
   c. I've been so captured by God's goodness and joy that it simply overflows in a desire to give.

2. I choose where to give based on:
   a. Whoever asks me to give.
   b. Things that have impacted me and causes I am attracted to.
   c. My view of things that matter to God.

3. When I give:
   a. I am eager to be recognized for my generosity.
   b. I love knowing I've had an impact and am part of something bigger.
   c. I truly want the glory to go to God, not me. I've given anonymous gifts.

4. The amount I give is:
   a. 0–10 percent.
   b. 10–15 percent.
   c. 15–20 percent or more.

5. When it comes to making a big, scary, faith-filled gift:
   a. I've never quite taken a step like that. (If this is you, stay tuned for the conclusion!)
   b. I've done that once or twice.
   c. That has been part of my journey multiple times.

6. When it comes to planning my giving:
   a. It's mostly haphazard.
   b. I have some regular schedules and places where I give, but no long-term plan.
   c. I have a clear, longer-term vision for my generosity and the impact I hope it will have.

7. The organizations I give to:

    a. Are somewhat random.

    b. Are primarily gospel-centered and mostly effective in their work.

    c. Are advancing God's kingdom effectively and include my local church.

8. When it comes to talking about generosity with others:

    a. Giving is a private matter between me and my immediate family.

    b. I've shared mutual encouragement in the area of generosity with close friends.

    c. I talk openly about the joy of generosity with others, because it's a critical part of the discipleship journey for every Christian.

9. I give because I want to:

    a. Pay it forward.

    b. Honor God and be faithful.

    c. Invest in eternal rewards and experience the joy of a closer relationship with God.

10. The top benefit I receive from giving is:

    a. A sense of fulfilled duty.

    b. The joy of generosity as I take part in making the world better.

    c. My own spiritual formation as I conform to the image of Christ.

Add up your answer choices! Whichever answer choice receives the most votes represents roughly where you are in the giving journey. Write your scores below or in your journal, and circle the stage you are in. Note that this is just a fun, lighthearted diagnostic tool, and even extravagant givers have lots of opportunity to grow.

Choice	Number	Stage
a		Emerging Giver
b		Committed Giver
c		Extravagant Giver

As you think about this quiz, are there any actions that come to mind as a next step in your own giving journey with God? If so, write them down here or in your journal.

_____

_____

_____

_____

_____

_____

_____

_____

_____

_____

_____

_____

CONCLUSION
The True Riches Challenge

If then you have not been faithful in the unrighteous wealth, who will entrust to you the true riches?

—Jesus, Luke 16:11

WHAT NOW? WE hope this book has made it clear that God doesn't have a list of financial rules for you to follow. Rather than sending us a rulebook, God came to us as a person, Jesus. And he's invited us to become his disciples and friends. As we wrap up this book, we want to pause to consider his invitation to gain a closer relationship with him through our money.

FINANCIAL DISCIPLESHIP

As we saw in the introduction, money can derail us spiritually, even if we are "succeeding" financially. How can we get on the right track? This book outlined four transformations from God for our financial lives—transformations that lead to true riches. Our pride becomes gratitude as we remember that everything we have, including our salvation, is a gift from God. Our coveting becomes contentment as our spending takes on the healthy boundaries of margin and "enough." Our anxiety becomes trust as we allow God to be our provider, even as we save money for the future. And, finally, our indifference becomes love as giving transforms our hearts to become more like God's, full of overwhelming love for others.

This is truly a joyful road and truly a hard road. It's like climbing Mount Everest: the thrill of a lifetime but also a costly and difficult endeavor, full of setbacks and challenges. The Christian road to life and joy passes through the cross, and our finances have to go to the cross with us. But it's absolutely worthwhile. Many times we'll have exhilarating joy and peace, as we stand on top of the world. But occasionally we'll have tears, doubt, and heartache, when we're at twenty-six thousand feet and can't see through the snowstorm all around us. Jesus said, "For the gate is narrow and the way is hard that leads to life, and those who find it are few."[1] But through it all, God is with us and sustains us with a deep peace. Jesus knows the way and guarantees that if we follow him, we'll make it up the mountain.

THE INVITATION TO GIVE IN THREE SCRIPTURES

First Timothy 6:18–19 is one of the best summary statements for God's invitation to those who have financial resources.

> They are to do good, to be rich in good works, to be generous and ready to share, thus storing up treasure

for themselves as a good foundation for the future,
so that they may take hold of that which is truly life.

According to this passage, we don't give because we're supposed to. Rather, we give in pursuit of something great. God holds out true riches—a meaningful life of gratitude, contentment, trust, and love, alongside eternal rewards—and asks us how much we'd like to buy. It's an awesome opportunity!

The prophet Isaiah elaborated on this point, describing how God will stand behind and guide his generous givers.

Share your bread with the hungry and bring the
homeless poor into your house . . . [and] the glory of
the LORD shall be your rear guard. . . .

If you pour yourself out for the hungry and satisfy
the desire of the afflicted, then shall your light rise
in the darkness and your gloom be as the noonday.
And the LORD will guide you continually . . .[2]

Our giving buys us true riches, and as a bonus God himself will guard us from behind and lead us from ahead.

Not only does our giving draw us closer to God, it also creates an impact here on earth. Our giving can change history as we partner with God in his work. The apostle Paul gave us a rallying cry to this end:

How then will they call on him in whom they have
not believed? And how are they to believe in him of

whom they have never heard? And how are they to hear without someone preaching? And how are they to preach unless they are sent?[3]

Without generous givers standing behind them, missionaries cannot complete the task to which they've been called by God. Without financial resources, ministries dedicated to clothing and feeding the poor in Jesus' name cannot operate. Without faithful supporters, churches cannot disciple and build up the body of Christ. We have an opportunity to fund the greatest project in the history of the world. God lets us help him build his kingdom!

Let's rally together, and let's get the job done. Extreme poverty could be wiped off the face of planet Earth in our lifetime. The last Bible translator may have already been born. We live in amazing times, and God has allowed us to live in such a time as this for a reason and a purpose.

The True Riches Challenge is designed to be a first step toward accepting God's invitation to build his kingdom and grow closer to Christ. Diving into giving, like any aspect of serious discipleship, is a heart-pumping moment. But you were made in the image of God, who is himself a giver. If you're a Christian, you have the spiritual DNA of Jesus—you were literally designed to be a giver!

This challenge should take only ten to fifteen minutes to complete. Please approach it prayerfully and be prepared to listen for God's guidance. If you're married, you may want to complete it as a couple.

Let's get started.

THE TRUE RICHES CHALLENGE

The True Riches Challenge is to make a gift to one of the three big tasks: a gift that gets your heart racing and makes you nervously excited about stepping into God's economy. We've split the process into three easy steps.

First, *discern before God the timing and size of your gift.* You can choose to give now as a lump sum, or commit to reaching a giving goal within the next year.

We suggest considering a goal equal to or larger than your biggest gift ever, but any faith-filled number that is both possible and also challenging will work. It shouldn't be an impossible gift for you, but it shouldn't be easy. The number should make you slightly nervous.

Circle the timing and number that you have selected, or write them down in your journal.

Second, *consider where to give.* Start by choosing one of the three main tasks God has given to us. God may invite you to double down on the task you've already invested a lot in before, or he might challenge you to try something new in order to form your heart to become more like his. Remember, through your gift God is inviting you into a closer relationship with him.

Timing
Now
Within One Year
Size
$500
$1,000
$2,000
$5,000
$10,000
$20,000
$50,000
$100,000
Other

Choose the task below into which you feel God would like you to invest your gift, and circle it or write it down in your journal.

Serve the Poor   Save the Lost   Strengthen Believers

Once you select the task you'd like to invest in, you'll then select an organization. This could be your local church, or it might be another ministry or even an individual. Selecting an organization might seem challenging. Don't give up! Job reflected on his own generosity, saying, "I searched out the cause of him whom I did not know."[4]

You may already know a great organization you'll give to, or you might choose to start with some internet research, or you might want to ask your pastor or a trusted friend for some advice. It's worth the effort to make a choice. Like Job, let's search out the cause of people we don't even know, for Jesus.

The organization I'll give to:

_____

Third, *share the joy of generosity with others.* Scripture tells us to let our light shine before others, so that they will give glory to God. With a posture of humility and gratitude to God, share the story of your financial journey and your True Riches Challenge with a trusted friend, your small group, or a mentor. In whatever way works best for you, invite someone else into your journey. You've chosen to swim upstream and to follow Christ financially, but there are many people who simply don't know about God's financial invitation to abundant life. Help spread the word!

YOUR NEXT STEP

Now that you've chosen your amount and timing and have chosen a task and perhaps an organization, it's time to act. Ask God to give you courage as you make this large, faith-filled gift, and ask him to shape your heart to be more like his.

Feel free to write some practical notes below or in your journal about how you'll execute this gift or share your journey in community.

Do you need to speak to a trusted advisor about where to give? Build a cashflow plan that creates the margin needed to fund this gift over the next year? Share a copy of this book with someone else? Sell some stocks? Write a check? Schedule coffee with a friend to share your generosity journey? Jot down some ideas.

Now, this book is over. But, praise God, your life is not. What will you do to take hold of true riches in your life journey, with the days you have left on planet Earth? We pray that you'll experience the gratitude, contentment, trust, and love of a life fully surrendered to the good purposes of your Father in heaven.

SMALL GROUP STUDY OUTLINE

WE ARE NOT meant to live the Christian life on our own. We see in Acts 2 the value of engaging in our faith with other followers of Christ. You may have experienced this firsthand via your local church, Bible studies, community groups, etc. This same principle also applies to our finances: engaging in stewardship alongside our faith community allows us to better experience the joy of generosity and to better connect with fellow believers.

We have created a four-week small group study guide to accompany this book. We encourage readers to progress through this study guide alongside a small group of fellow Christians. We believe God uses such groups to provide a deeper understanding of his teaching and to enable more practical discussion on how to apply his lessons in our daily lives. May God grant you the opportunity to experience *true riches*—gratitude, contentment, trust, and love—in your life, for his glory!

The four-week small group reading schedule is below:

Meeting 1: Intro, Chapter 1, Chapter 2
Meeting 2: Chapter 3
Meeting 3: Chapter 4
Meeting 4: Chapter 5 and Conclusion

GROUP SESSION: INTRO, CHAPTER 1, AND CHAPTER 2

Introductions

- Each person share: What is your name, and what is one memory you have of money from before the age of twelve?

Video Story

- Watch the video "Work Like a Doctor, Live Like a Nurse" on www.truerichesbook.com to see the story of one doctor, Renee Lockey, who experienced a radical transformation in her perspective on money.

Discussion of Video Story

- What stood out to you in the story?
- How does Renee's journey demonstrate the relationship between gratitude and our finances?

Discussion and Reflection

- Each person share: What is one thing that stood out to you as you read the introduction and chapters 1 and 2 and completed the reflection?
- Action Steps: Think of three aspects of your life for which you are most grateful. You might think of relationships, possessions, or experiences. To whom are you grateful for these things? Take time to thank that person and express your gratitude.
- Conclude in prayer, and discuss time and location of next session.

GROUP SESSION: CHAPTER 3

Welcome Question

- Think about your whole life. In what season of life were you most content? At that time, did you have more possessions, or fewer, than you do now?

Video Story

- Watch the video "Tom and Bree Hsieh" on www.truerichesbook.com.

Discussion of Video Story

- What stood out to you in the story?
- How does the Hsieh family's journey demonstrate the power of contentment to produce both joy and fruit for God's kingdom?

Discussion and Reflection

- Each person share: What is one thing that stood out to you as you read chapter 3 and completed the reflection?
- Action Steps: What is one financial category in your life where you are either struggling to have enough margin (that is, it is stretching your budget) or you are struggling to decide how much is "enough" (perhaps you're still striving for more and more)? Brainstorm what resources you might seek out this week to provide additional clarity on this topic—it might be a wise individual or advisor, a book, or some other resource.
- Conclude in prayer, and discuss time and location of next session.

GROUP SESSION: CHAPTER 4

Welcome Question

- What are you most anxious about today when it comes to money?

Video Story

- Watch the video "Jimmy and Laura Seibert" on www.truerichesbook.com.

Discussion of Video Story

- What stood out to you in the story?
- How does the Seibert family's journey demonstrate the power of trust to produce both joy and fruit for God's kingdom?

Discussion and Reflection

- Each person share: What is one thing that stood out to you as you read chapter 4 and completed the reflection?
- Action Steps: What financial decision or obligation do you currently face that causes you the most stress and anxiety? Share your experience with each other as a group. Brainstorm a small step you might take this week to alleviate your anxiety about this issue and further trust in God as your provider.
- Conclude in prayer, and discuss time and location of next session.

GROUP SESSION: CHAPTER 5 AND CONCLUSION

Welcome Question

- What is the most loving act of generosity you have ever witnessed?

Video Story

- Watch the video teaching "Overflow of Joy" from John Piper on www.truerichesbook.com.

Discussion of Video Story

- What stood out to you in the teaching?
- How does this message connect with what you learned in chapter 5?

Discussion and Reflection

- Each person share: What is one thing that stood out to you as you read chapter 5 and completed the reflection?
- Action Steps: complete the *True Riches* Challenge found in the conclusion. To which area of giving do you feel most called (Serve the Poor, Save the Lost, or Strengthen Believers)? What makes you excited to support God's work in this area? Discuss as a group why you are passionate about this area and discuss how you may choose to support this area going forward.
- Conclude in prayer.

ADDITIONAL RESOURCES

COURSES AND EXPERIENCES
On Generosity
- *Embark: Discerning Next Steps in Your Generosity Journey* is a free online course from Generous Giving. Details can be found at www.generousgiving.org /embark.

On Biblical Personal Finance
- *Compass: Finances God's Way* is a comprehensive course on all aspects of personal finance from a biblical perspective. www.compass1.org.

BOOKS
- *On Social Justice*, St. Basil the Great
- *On Wealth and Poverty*, John Chrysostom
- *Your Money Counts*, Howard Dayton
- *The Treasure Principle*, Randy Alcorn
- *Money, Possessions, and Eternity*, Randy Alcorn
- *Abundant*, Todd Harper
- *God and Money*, John Cortines and Gregory Baumer

ACKNOWLEDGMENTS

THERE ARE FAR too many wonderful leaders to thank, and we have far too little space to say "thank you." To everyone who has aided our journey, please accept our humbled, heartfelt gratitude.

Todd Harper, thank you for your consistent and godly leadership that has shaped our lives in many ways. To the entire team at Generous Giving, thank you for sharing with many, including us, that giving brings joy and is something God wants for us, not from us.

Howard Dayton, thank you for your loving mentorship. You've left a bigger mark than you'll ever know.

To every countercultural, biblical voice who has shaped our perspectives, thank you for your faithfulness. Specifically, Randy Alcorn, Francis Chan, David Platt, John Piper, Jeff Manion, Andy Stanley, and many others, thank you for investing your lives into biblical truth on money and passing it along to our generation.

To one anonymous couple, our Gospel Patrons and unbelievable supporters, your generosity models what we've talked about in this book and, in so many ways, has made possible all that God has chosen to do in and through our lives.

Dr. Rob Plummer and Dr. Ruth Anne Reese, thank you for serving as our theological auditors and providing early manuscript input. We are not trained Bible scholars, but we're deeply committed to engaging with God's Word faithfully. Thus, your partnership as biblical scholars was vital. Your feedback, coaching, and guidance ensured that we business guys stayed as close to the biblical bull's-eye as possible.

Jeff Barneson and Mark Washington, thank you both for faithfully encouraging MBA students to seek after Jesus in your ministry at InterVarsity. You have impacted both of our spiritual trajectories for the better.

Heartfelt thanks to Jessica Wong for your outstanding editorial work on this manuscript and to the whole team at Thomas Nelson. Dan Balow and Steve Laube, our literary agents, and all the others involved in the literary process.

Finally, we'd like to thank those who specifically gave their expertise and commentary as we brainstormed and envisioned this project throughout 2017. Your names are below, and your input was tremendous!

Rob Plummer	Janice Munemitsu
Mac South	Allan Samson
Tony Cimmarrusti	Mark D. Pflug
Jason Coffey	Lee Behar
Jason Pappas	Keith Phillips
Dan Glaze	Zane Henderson
Melinda Eller	Peter Greer
Dave Briggs	Lee Turner
Evan Lenow	Heather McGill
Adam Miller	Ray Pertierra

Justin Murff

Lacie Stevens

Terry Johnson

Brett Whitley

Sharon Epps

Jeff Ryan

Roger Lam

Jessica Pappas

Gunnar Johnson

Emily Vogelzang Murray

Pearl Ko

Denis Beausejour

Matt Burton

Kirk and Cindy Flanegan

Al Mueller

Blair Graham

Todd Harper

Heather Tuininga

Jim Rathbun

Tony Wilks

Matt Massey

Ty Osman

Shane Enete

Stephen Kump

Amy Chiu

Aaron Still

Trish Crossley

Isaac Ezell

Stephen Reiff

D. Scott Luttrell

Steve Carter

Megan Cortines

Steve Reiff

Howard Dayton

Chris White

Jeff Merkler

Ryan Kaczmarek

Hunter Wharton

Barry McCall

Rich VanderSande

Eric Hoffman

Jeff Kahler

JR Cifani

Todd Dekruyter

NOTES

Introduction
1. See Matt. 13:44, which has become my life verse.

Chapter 1: The Big Question
1. Some teachers have cited Luke 14:28 in support of saving money, since Jesus remarks that anyone building a tower should count the cost. In fact, this is the opposite of what Jesus meant. The quote in question is part of Jesus' explanation of the cost of discipleship. The metaphor of the tower illustrates the all-in sacrifice disciples must make, and Jesus continues in the same paragraph with, "So therefore, any one of you who does not renounce all that he has cannot be my disciple." This is hardly an encouragement to save money!
2. Matt. 6:24.
3. The encounter, with which we have taken poetic license, is recorded in Luke 16:14–15.

Chapter 2: From Pride to Gratitude
1. C. S. Lewis, *Mere Christianity* (New York: HarperCollins, 2001), 125.
2. Rom. 3:23.
3. He wrote roughly half of the psalms in the Bible.
4. 1 Chron. 21:1–4.
5. Jeff Manion, *Satisfied* (Grand Rapids: Zondervan, 2013), chap. 18.
6. Rev. 3:15–17, 19–20, emphasis added.
7. See 1 Sam. 16 for the scriptural basis behind our rendering of this tale.

8. Luke 15:11–32.
9. Luke 15:20–24.
10. Luke 6:45.
11. Deut. 8:17–18. Prior to these verses Moses spells out the coming blessings: multiplying silver and gold, new homes, growing agricultural output, and even a healthy copper mining industry.
12. 1 Chron. 29:11–15.
13. Jer. 9:23–24.
14. Dan. 4:30 (The Message).

Chapter 3: From Coveting to Contentment

1. Eph. 5:5.
2. Heb. 13:4–5.
3. Ambrose of Milan, *The Fathers of the Church*, trans. John J. Savage, vol. 42, *Hexameron, Paradise, and Cain and Abel* (Washington DC: CUA Press, 2010), 379.
4. N. T. Wright, *Paul: A Biography* (Read by James Langton. New York: HarperAudio, 2018), Audible audio ed., 15 hr., 22 min.
5. Matt. 13:22.
6. Luke 12:15.
7. St. Basil the Great, *On Social Justice* (Yonkers, NY: St. Vladimir's Seminary Press, 2009), 48.
8. 1 Tim. 6:6–10.
9. 1 Tim. 5:8.
10. Walter Brueggemann, *Money and Possessions* (Louisville: Westminster John Knox Press, 2016), 15.
11. Eccl. 5:10 (niv).
12. Phil. 4:11–13.
13. Paul had been a top student under the most famous rabbi of his day, Gamaliel.
14. Wess Stafford, *Too Small to Ignore: Why the Least of These Matters Most* (Colorado Springs: Waterbrook Press, 2007), 165 (emphasis original).
15. 1 Thess. 1:6–7.
16. 2 Cor. 8:2.

17. As remembered from a sermon by Dr. Joel Hunter, Northland Church, 2017.
18. Rom. 6:4.
19. Dietrich Bonhoeffer, *The Cost of Discipleship* (New York: Simon & Schuster, 1995), 89.
20. See the story of the young ruler: Mark 10:17–31.
21. See the story of Zacchaeus: Luke 19:1–10.
22. Matt. 13:44–46.
23. Lev. 19:9–10.
24. Matt. 13:22.
25. As a family of four and subject to inflation adjustments over time.
26. Key factors that may impact your family's decision on how much is "enough" include: the geography where you live, the number of dependents (children, aging parents, etc.) for whom you provide care, health status, hobbies and interests, etc. There is no single formula that spits out the answer for each family, but we do believe that God will faithfully guide you toward the right number for your family if you engage with him on this topic.
27. Not all of this comes from his nonprofit salary. This also includes book royalties and advances, speaking and preaching honorariums, and board membership earnings.
28. Randy Alcorn, *Money, Possessions, and Eternity*, rev. ed. (Carol Stream, IL: Tyndale, 2003), 289.

Chapter 4: From Anxiety to Trust

1. D. Kahneman and A. Tversky, "Choices, Values, and Frames," *American Psychologist* 39, no. 4 (1984): 341–50.
2. "Stress in America ™ Press Room," American Psychological Association, updated January 24, 2018, http://www.apa.org/news/press/releases/stress/.
3. Matt. 6:31, 33.
4. Luke 12:32.
5. Luke 18:21–23.
6. Luke 19:9.
7. Jer. 10:2, 5, 15.
8. Prov. 23:4–5.

9. Eccl. 5:12.
10. Ps. 37:4.
11. The Beatles, "Can't Buy Me Love," by Lennon-McCartney, released March 16, 1964, Capitol Records, 7 rpm.
12. "Buy Me a Boat," MP3 audio, track 1 on Chris Janson, *Buy Me a Boat*, Warner Bros., 2015.
13. Ylan Q. Mui, "The Shocking Number of Americans Who Can't Cover a $400 Expense," *Washington Post*, May 25, 2016, https://www.washingtonpost.com/news/wonk/wp/2016/05/25/the-shocking-number-of-americans-who-cant-cover-a-400-expense/?utm_term=.5df198ec65f4.
14. Rick Warren, "Trust: God Cares About Your Bills," PastorRick.com, accessed January 15, 2018, http://pastorrick.com/devotional/english/trust-god-cares-about-your-bills.
15. Luke 12:22–23.
16. Referencing Phil. 4:12.
17. Warren, "Trust: God Cares About Your Bills."
18. Julia Zorthian, "Most Americans Are Losing Sleep Over Money Concerns," *TIME*, April 20, 2017, http://time.com/money/4749161/americans-insomnia-health-care-insurance-costs/.
19. Luke 12:16–21.
20. Please note that the rich fool in Luke 12 is different from the rich young ruler in Luke 18, who is different from the rich man in Luke 16. Hmm . . . maybe Jesus was trying to make a point with all these stories about rich people who failed spiritually!
21. Prov. 21:20.
22. Heb. 13:20–21.
23. "FAQs: Global Poverty Line Update," The World Bank, September 30, 2015, http://www.worldbank.org/en/topic/poverty/brief/global-poverty-line-faq; Jessica L. Semega, Kayla R. Fontenot, and Melissa A. Kollar, "Income and Poverty in the United States: 2016," United States Census Bureau, September 12, 2017, https://census.gov/library/publications/2017/demo/p60-259.html.
24. Chasen Turk, "15 World Hunger Statistics," The Borgen

Project, March 15, 2017, https://borgenproject
.org/15-world-hunger-statistics/.

25. "Global Water, Sanitation, and Hygiene (WASH)," Centers for Disease Control and Prevention, last updated April 11, 2016, https://www.cdc.gov/healthywater/global/wash _statistics.html.

26. Deut. 15:11.

27. Josh. 21:45; Num. 23:19.

28. Isa. 63:9; 40:29 (second verse NIV).

29. 2 Cor. 1:3–4.

30. John 4:13–14.

31. James 1:2–4.

32. Isa. 58:7–8.

33. Phil. 4:19.

34. Randy Alcorn, *Managing God's Money* (Carol Stream, IL: Tyndale, 2011), 80.

35. Basil, *On Social Justice*, 83.

36. John Ronsvalle and Sylvia Ronsvalle, *The State of Church Giving* vol. 27, *Through 2015: Understanding the Times* (Champaign, IL: Empty Tomb Inc., 2017).

37. Christian Smith and Hilary Davidson, "Giving Makes Us Happy. So Why Do So Few Do It?" Science of Generosity, November 3, 2014, https://generosityresearch.nd.edu/news /giving-makes-us-happy-then-why-do-so-few-do-it/.

38. *The State of Church Giving Through 2016: What Do Denominational Leaders Want to Do with $368 Billion More a Year?* (Empty Tomb, Inc. 28th ed., 2018).

39. Randy Alcorn, "More Happy-Making to Give," Eternal Perspectives Ministries, March 29, 2010, http://www.epm .org/resources/2010/Mar/29/happy-making-video/.

40. Luke 6:38.

41. Matt. 19:21.

42. Matt. 6:19–21. Much more could be said on the subject of eternal rewards. For a fantastic study of the subject please see *The Law of Rewards* by Randy Alcorn.

43. 1 John 3:17.

44. Jer. 22:16.

45. Prov. 11:24–25. For clarity, this verse is *not* supporting a false

prosperity-gospel theology. God promises to bless us if we are generous, but those blessings may not be in the form of financial reward. They could be other blessings on earth such as stronger relationships or a greater sense of purpose, or we may not even experience the blessings until we are with God in heaven.

46. 2 Cor. 9:6–7.
47. Mark Lloydbottom, *Foundation Truth on Money and Possessions* (London: Your Money Counts, 2016), available from Compass (https://www .compass1.eu/): https://docs.wixstatic.com/ugd /dc8391_5f2c43805fd1497cb2bb980e6d385925.pdf.
48. Matt. 6:31–33.
49. Author Randy Alcorn offers this fantastic quote from church father Cyprian (c. AD 210–258) in *Money, Possessions, and Eternity*: "Their property held them in chains. . . . They think of themselves as owners, whereas it is they rather who are owned: enslaved as they are to their own property, they are not the masters of their money but its slaves" (p. 416).
50. Eccl. 5:10.
51. Richard J. Foster, *Celebration of Discipline: The Path to Spiritual Growth* (San Francisco: HarperOne, 1988), 88.
52. Check out the videos at the website I Like Giving (www .ilikegiving.org) to see inspiring examples of how God uses obedience in generosity to bless the *giver* just as much as the recipient!
53. 1 Peter 5:7 (NIV).
54. Walter Brueggemann, *Money and Possessions* (Louisville: Westminster John Knox Press, 2016), 196.
55. Prov. 6:6–8; 22:7.
56. Eccl. 5:13.
57. Luke 12:13–21.
58. Matt. 25:31–46.
59. Prov. 21:20.
60. Luke 12:13–21.
61. Emmanuel Saez and Gabriel Zucman, "Savings Rates by Wealth Class" graph, quoted in "The Average Savings Rates by Income (Wealth Class)," Financial Samurai, accessed

August 9, 2018, https://www.financialsamurai.com/
the-average-savings-rates-by-income-wealth-class/.

62. Brad Hewitt and James Moline, *Your New Money Mindset: Create a Healthy Relationship with Money* (Carol Stream, IL: Tyndale, 2015), 241 (notes on chapter two).

63. *Report on the Economic Well-Being of U.S. Households in 2017* (Washington, DC: Board of Governors of the Federal Reserve System, 2018), https://www.federalreserve.gov/publications/files/2017-report-economic-well-being-us-households-201805.pdf, 21. The study also found that 46 percent of American households cannot immediately come up with a spare $400 if faced with an emergency (21).

64. Prov. 22:7. As Basil of Caesarea wrote, "A father's debt leads into prison. Do not leave a bond, a paternal curse, as it were, descending upon the sons and grandsons" (*Homily* 12.4 on Psalm 14, from vol. 46 of *The Fathers of the Church* series).

65. A 2:1 ratio of mortgage loan to annual income may be challenging in certain geographies, especially large urban centers. If you live in such an area, we recommend seeking counsel from a trusted Christian financial advisor on what size mortgage loan is wise for you, but please know that exceeding this ratio will tie up a significantly large fraction of your income.

66. Amy L. Sherman, *Directions in Women's Giving 2012*, (Orlando: Women Doing Well, 2012), http://womendoingwell.org/about/research-new/.

67. If you want deeper guidance on managing long-term goals, consider locating a Christian financial advisor or enrolling in a Compass small group study. There are many complexities and nuances involved in financial planning that this book does not delve into.

Chapter 5: From Indifference to Love

1. Matt. 6:21.

2. Ola Svenson, "Are We All Less Risky and More Skillful Than Our Fellow Drivers?" Acta Psychologica 47, no. 2 (February 1981): 143–48, http://heatherlench.

com/wp-content/uploads/2008/07/svenson.pdf,
doi:10.1016/0001–6918(81)90005–6.

3. "The Generosity Gap," Barna Group with Thrivent Financial,
https://www.barna.com/generosity/. Left-hand column
includes those reporting themselves as "very" or "somewhat"
generous with money. Even more shockingly, only 2 percent
of millennial Christians gave more than $2,500 last year to
churches and charities.

4. Credit for this idea goes to Dollar Street (www.dollarstreet.
org). They have a large collection of photos from the real lives
of families around the world living on all points of the income
spectrum.

5. Data is PPP-adjusted to reflect different costs of living
around the world. This table is based on a family/household
size of three people; the figures will be slightly off, but still
illustrative, if your household size is smaller or larger. Global
Rich List, http://www.globalrichlist.com; Christoph Lakner
and Branko Milanovic, "Global Income Distribution: From
the Fall of the Berlin Wall to the Great Recession," The World
Bank, December 2013, http://documents.worldbank.org/
curated/en/914431468162277879/pdf/WPS6719.pdf; Rakesh
Kochhar, "A Global Middle Class Is More Promise Than
Reality," Pew Research Center, July 8, 2015, http://www
.pewglobal.org/2015/07/08/a-global-middle-class-is-more
-promise-than-reality/#who-is-middle-income.

6. 1 Tim. 6:17.

7. There is no specific rationale for the order of these tasks as
presented. All three are clear mandates of Scripture.

8. The parable of the sheep and the goats: Matt. 25:31–46.

9. James 1:27.

10. John Chrysostom, *On Wealth and Poverty* (Yonkers, NY:
St. Vladimir's Seminary Press, 1984).

11. Matt. 28:18–20.

12. Every Tribe Every Nation: Eradicating Biblical Poverty,
accessed August 9, 2018, www.everytribeeverynation.org.

13. The groundbreaking effort IllumiNations has been
undertaken by ten of the largest Bible translation agencies—
an effort to share data, collaborate toward the shared task

of ending Bible poverty, and allocate funds across different ministries according to their share of the greater mission. You can learn more about this effort at www.illuminations.bible.

14. David B. Barrett and Todd M. Johnson, *World Christian Trends, AD 30–AD 2200: Interpreting the Annual Christian Megacensus* (Pasadena, CA: William Carey Library, 2001), 655.
15. 1 Tim. 5:17–18.
16. Ps. 90:12.
17. 1 Tim. 6:19.
18. Matt. 19:30.
19. 1 Cor. 3:13–15 (THE MESSAGE).
20. Church fathers generally discounted the idea of giving in your will, saying that this was not *true* generosity. Social science research by the Science of Generosity Project at Notre Dame agrees, indicating that giving from one's will does not provide joy or fulfillment in the same way that normal giving does. Estate giving is better than nothing, but the best move is to give today, while we are still alive.
21. Sondra Ely Wheeler, *Wealth as Peril and Obligation: The New Testament on Possessions* (Grand Rapids: Eerdmans, 1995), 49.

Conclusion

1. Matt. 7:14.
2. Excerpts from Isa. 58. It is worth reading this whole chapter for a beautiful description of God's vision for giving.
3. Rom. 10:14–15.
4. Job 29:16.

ABOUT THE AUTHORS

JOHN CORTINES serves as chief operating officer at Generous Giving, a nonprofit that seeks to spread the biblical message of generosity. He holds an MBA from Harvard Business School and speaks regularly at churches and conferences around the country. John and his wife, Megan, have three children and reside in Orlando, Florida.

GREG BAUMER serves as chief growth officer at navi-Health, a healthcare technology company. He holds a BS from Indiana University and an MBA from Harvard Business School and speaks regularly at churches and conferences around the country. Greg and his wife, Alison, have three children and reside in Nashville, Tennessee.